GLOCK

The New Wave in Combat Handguns

PETER ALAN KASLER

PALADIN PRESS
BOULDER, COLORADO

Also by Peter Alan Kasler:

Business Partners: The Best Pistol/Ammunition
  Combinations for Personal Defense

Glock: The New Wave in Combat Handguns
by Peter Alan Kasler

Copyright © 1992 Peter Alan Kasler

ISBN 0-87364-649-5
Printed in the United States of America

Published by Paladin Press, a division of
Paladin Enterprises, Inc., P.O. Box 1307,
Boulder, Colorado 80306, USA.
(303) 443-7250

Direct inquiries and/or orders to the above address.

Visit our Web site at www.paladin-press.com

CONTENTS

ACKNOWLEDGMENTS

In addition to thanking Gaston Glock for sharing the fruits of his brilliance with us all, I wish to acknowledge those who provided assistance and support in the writing of this book:

Karl F. Walter, executive vice president of Glock, Inc., not only personally provided information, materials, and support, he made it possible for others at Glock to do so as well.

Al Bell, director of training of Glock, Inc. tolerated my numerous questions and requests with unflagging good humor. Insisting that it was only his job, he made it considerably easier to do mine.

Bob Gates, national sales manager; Jim McNally, assistant manager, law enforcement services; Andra Ahn, customer service supervisor; and other people at Glock, Inc. all provided invaluable assistance and support during the writing of this book.

Many others helped by providing information, materials, and other necessary things so that this book could become a reality:

My good friend Massad Ayoob, who cheerfully and professionally accepted my criticisms and acknowledged that authorities can disagree in good faith.

A certain California Highway Patrol officer who asked to remain anonymous.

My friends at CATco.

My dear friends Brian Ehrmantraut and Moana Kutsche.

José Fernandez of JAF Gunsmithing, Inc.

The folks at Hesco, in LaGrange, Georgia.

John R. (Randy) Lamson, Jr., director of photography for NRA Publications and *American Rifleman*.

My friend Azad H. Nejad, owner of Photo Exchange in San Francisco, whose patience and good nature made my often poor photography acceptable.

Phil Levy of MP Research, Inc., in Victorville, California.

Carlos Santizo of U.S.A. Magazines (Clips).

Stephen T. Schwarzmann, marketing & strategic development manager of astrophysics Research Corporation.

Dave Shroka of Indelible, Inc., advertising and media information services for Glock, Inc.

The folks at Trijicon, Inc., in Farmington Hills, Michigan.

And countless others, though unnamed here, whose contributions are appreciated.

To Gaston Glock, who made it all possible.

GLOCK PISTOL SPECIFICATIONS

	17	17L	18	19	20	21	22	23
Caliber	9mm	9mm	9mm	9mm	10mm	.45ACP	.40 S&W	.40 S&W
Pistol wgt. empty, no magazine	21.91	23.35	23.00 +/- 1	20.99	26.35	25.22	22.36	20.67
Length overall (slide)	7.21	8.77	7.21	6.74	8.27	8.27	7.40	6.97
Height	5.16	5.16	5.16	4.92	5.16	6.16	5.16	4.92
Width	1.18	1.18	1.18	1.18	1.24	1.24	1.18	1.18
Sight Radius	6.50	8.03	6.50	5.98	6.77	6.77	6.50	5.98
Barrel Length	4.49	6.02	4.49	4.02	4.60	4.60	4.49	4.02
Barrel Rifling	Hex	Hex	Hex	Hex	Hex	Oct	Hex	Hex
Direction	R/H	R/H	R/H	R/H	R/H	R/H	R/H	R/H
Length of Twist	9.84	9.84	9.84	9.84	15.75	15.75	15.75	15.75
Cycle Rate	N/A	N/A	1150 +/- 50	N/A	N/A	N/A	N/A	N/A
Magazine Capacity Standard	17	17	17	15	15	13	15	13
Magazine Capacity Optional	19	19	19	17	17	15	17	15

Notes: All dimensions in inches unless otherwise noted.
All weights in ounces unless otherwise noted.

CHAPTER 1

Genesis and History of the Glock Dynasty

ome might say Deutsch-Wagram is nothing more than a suburb of Austria's magnificent capital, Vienna. A little town of barely 4,500 people, Deutsch-Wagram is only ten miles from Vienna's center and is nearly engulfed by its northeastern border, despite actually lying across it in the province of Lower Austria. Yes, some might say Deutsch-Wagram is nothing more than a suburb of Vienna, but those who would say that don't know about Gaston Glock.

During the 1950s Gaston Glock was an engineer working as plant manager for a manufacturing firm in his native Austria. In 1963 he struck out on his own, forming Glock Ges. m.b.H., a company that manufactured such things as doorknobs and hinges for the Austrian market. As time passed, Glock developed a variety of military- and police-related products, including military knives, entrenching tools, training and fragmentation hand grenades, and nondisintegrating machine gun belts.

It is doubtful if Gaston Glock realized then that a mere two decades later he would be the ruler of a firearms dynasty. Those in the cliquish firearms community certainly had not heard the name Glock, but if they had, they'd never have thought to rank it with such giants as Browning, Colt, Luger, Mauser, Kalashnikov, and Smith & Wesson. But soon the firearms world would do just that.

In 1980 the Austrian army began looking for a state-of-the-art 9mm Parabellum pistol, designated the P-80. They wanted to select one with which to equip their troops by 1983. Glock became aware of the army's search and impending procurement contract, and in 1982 he assembled a panel of Europe's best handgun experts from the law enforcement, military, and civilian sectors. From their input he developed a list of desirable features and characteristics for a modern semiautomatic handgun.

Next, the Austrian army's P-80 pistol test "limiting criteria" list was consulted to ensure that the proposed pistol would comply. The list consisted of seventeen criteria, reproduced here in the exact form and (translated) words of the Republic of Austria's Ministry of Defense:

1. The system has to be a self-loading pistol.
2. The pistol must be able to fire 9 mm S-round/P-08 (parabellum).
3. The filling of the magazine must be possible without any auxiliary means.
4. The magazine must have a minimum capacity of 8 rounds.
5. All manipulations for
   - preparation for firing
   - firing itself and
   - manipulation of the pistol after firing must be done single-handed, by choice right-handed as well as left-handed. [Author's note: This criterion required that the pistol be capable of being fired with one hand only. While designed primarily for right-handed shooters, it should be capable of being fired left-handed as well.]
6. The technical security of the pistol has to be unlimited guaranteed [absolutely guaranteed]

under any circumstances as they are
- shock
- stroke
- and dropping from a height of 2 m
[meters] on a steel plate.

7. Dismantling of the main parts of the pistol for cleaning and reassembling must be possible without any tools.
8. Maintaining and cleaning of the pistol must be possible without any tools.
9. The components of the pistol must not exceed more than 58 parts (equivalent of a pistol P-38).
10. Gages, measuring and testing devices must not be necessary for the long-term maintaining [for long-term maintenance].
11. The producer has to provide the Armed Forces at least at the time of the supplying of the pistol series with a complete set of drawings and exploded views. The drawings have to show measurements, tolerances, used material, surface treatment, and all necessary details for the production of the pistol.
12. All component parts must be exchangeable without any adjustment.
13. In firing the first 10,000 rounds (ammunition according to valid TL- [an Austrian firearms standards organization] regulations) not more than 20 jams are permitted, even if there would be no tools necessary for repairing. [No more than twenty jams are permitted during the first 10,000 rounds fired, and all jams are to be counted, including those that can be cleared without resorting to the use of tools.]
14. Supply of all main parts must be secured after 15,000 rounds load with ordinary ammunition and excess pressure test cartridge to maintain the security of further use of the pistol, techni-

cally and functionally. The excess pressure test cartridge has to have, according to valid regulations, a pressure of 5000 bar. [After firing 15,000 rounds of ordinary ammunition, the test pistol will be examined and all main parts must be securely in place. Then, after being subjected to a special test cartridge that generates 5,000 bar (considerably greater than normal pressure), the main parts must continue to function properly and meet technical specifications. Unless the test pistol meets these requirements, testing cannot continue.]

15. When [the gun is] properly handled the user must under no circumstances be endangered by the case ejection.

16. The muzzle energy must be at least 441,5 (J) when firing a 9 mm S-round/P-08 Hirtenberger Patronen AG.

17. Pistols achieving less than 70% of the maximum points will not be released for military use.

Armed with the list from his distinguished panel, and using modern manufacturing methods and nonstrategic materials such as polymer, Glock developed a working prototype suitable for submission to the Austrian army in only three months. Gaston Glock was the first person to successfully produce a polymer pistol receiver combined with a strong steel slide and barrel. And it was cost-effective to boot.

He submitted several test samples of the prototype Glock Model 17 9mm x 19 pistol to the Austrian army in early 1982. Later that year the Austrian Ministry of Defense notified Glock that the Model 17 had passed stringent testing procedures and bested all domestic and foreign competitors (eight other pistols submitted by five other manufacturers). Thus, the Austrian army selected the Glock Model 17 as its new service pistol; the initial order was for twenty-five thousand guns.

Gaston Glock examining a partially disassembled Model 17. (Photo courtesy of Randy Lamson of the National Rifle Association.)

COMPARISON CHART OF MAIN COMPETITORS
(Classified, for internal use only)

COUNTRY OF ORIGIN	MODEL DENOM. 9mm Para.	MAGAZINE CAPACITY	NUMBER OF COMPONENTS	WEIGHT Empty Mag. (g)	SLIDE MFG. TECHNOLOGY	CONVENT. DOUBLE (D)/ SINGLE (S) ACTION	OTHER TRIGGER/ COCKING-SYSTEM	LOCKING SYSTEM	RANKING AUSTRIAN ARMY TEST
HECKLER & KOCH FRG	P7	8	49	882	machined/welded	—	grip cocking	gas pressure retarded	
	P7A13	13	49 appr.	900 appr.	machined/welded	—	grip cocking	mass locking	
	P95	9	77	928	pressed sheet/welded	D/S	—	roller locking	
SIG – SAUER SWITZ	P220	9	53	818	pressed sheet/welded, rivetted	D/S	—	mechanical locking	
	P226	15 (using Beretta mag.)	58	845	pressed sheet/welded/ rivetted	D/S	—	mechanical locking	
BERETTA ITALY	92SB-F	15	70	975	cast machined	D/S	—	mechanical locking	
FN BELGIUM	FN35	**CONFIDENTIAL FOR INTERNAL USE ONLY**							
STEYR AUSTRIA	GB	18	49	1100	**DUPLICATION NOT PERMITTED**	D/S	—	gas pressure retarded mass locking	
GLOCK AUSTRIA	GLOCK 17	17 (18) 18 rounds loadable	34	661	machined from one solid rolled steel bar, no weld./rivetting	—	new "Safe Action" system, constant trigger pull, 3 auto safeties	mechanical locking	1

Included in the letter containing the good news from the Austrian Ministry of Defense was this comparison chart of the Glock Model 17 and its main competitors.

6

Since late 1982 the Glock Model 17 pistol has been available on the West European market, as well as to Western law enforcement and military agencies wishing to obtain test samples.

Between 1982 and 1985, thirty-six U.S. firearms importers contacted Glock Ges. m.b.H. seeking to obtain exclusive importation rights for the Model 17. Included among these were companies that marketed competitive firearms and the U.S. Department of Defense (DOD), which inquired about the pistol in late 1983 and received four samples for unofficial evaluation.

Shortly thereafter the DOD invited Glock to participate in the 1984 XM-9 Personal Defense Pistol Trials (which ultimately resulted in the Beretta submission being selected as the official sidearm of the U.S. military, replacing the venerable Colt 1911A1). Glock declined because it was not possible to retool existing production equipment and build thirty-five test samples that would meet DOD criteria in time to participate.

In 1984 and 1985 Norway and Sweden jointly tested several modern sidearms then available from various Western nations. Following extensive trials, both of these nations selected the Glock Model 17 for military use. It had surpassed all prior NATO durability and strength standards. As a result, the Model 17 became a standard NATO-classified and adopted sidearm (NATO Stock No. 1005/25/133/6775).

Beginning in 1984, the pistol became the choice of various presidential and head-of-state guard units (Syria, Jordan, the Venezuelan CAVIM Commandos, the Philippine Presidential Guard, India's Special Protection Guard, etc.) and world-renowned antiterrorist units (Germany's famed GSG 9, Austria's Cobra Unit, the Q.P.P. Sûreté du Quebec Tactical Unit, the Royal Canadian Mounted Police Urge Team, etc.). Early law enforcement customers were the Austrian Federal Police and the Schaerbeek, Belgium, Police Department. During the same time period, the Model 17 was gaining interest in the Western law enforcement community.

In July 1985, a Glock Model 17 was submitted to the Bureau of Alcohol, Tobacco and Firearms (BATF) for importation evaluation because Glock, after assessing and evaluating the U.S. market, had begun plans to come to America. To satisfy BATF, two changes were necessary: 1) a metal serial number plate installed on the underside of the polymer receiver, just forward of the trigger guard; and 2) an adjustable rear sight to replace the fixed rear sight.

The metal serial number plate on the receiver's underside was required because BATF insists that pistols have their serial numbers permanently affixed in several specific places, one of which is on the receiver. As no satisfactory method existed of stamping or otherwise emblazoning the number on the polymer receiver, it was agreed that a metal plate with the serial number stamped on it would be permanently affixed.

Many people have heard the adjustable rear sight referred to as the "weekend sight" because Gaston Glock reputedly designed it over a weekend, but few understand why an adjustable sight was necessary to meet BATF's importation criteria. Well, here's the answer: BATF has a points system for importation criteria; all pistols must achieve seventy-four points (awarded for various features on the pistol) to qualify. Partly because it is so light (pistols get two points per ounce, and the Model 17 weighs only 21.91 ounces empty without a magazine installed), the original Model 17 came up just short on points.

Evidently, replacing the fixed rear sight with an adjustable one was the best solution for two reasons: it brought the point total up sufficiently to comply with

BATF importation requirements, and it didn't necessitate making any permanent or significant alteration to the near-perfect pistol.

The "famous" Glock adjustable, or "weekend," rear sight.

In November 1985 a second pistol was submitted, and verbal approval came in late November, with official documentation following on 10 January 1986.

Meanwhile, between July and November 1985, Gaston Glock and Glock Ges. m.b.H.'s marketing manager, Wolfgang Riedl, formed Glock, Inc. in the United States. The task of actually establishing Glock, Inc. and its U.S. location was assigned to Karl Walter, vice president. In November 1985, Smyrna, Georgia, a suburb of Atlanta, became Glock's American home. All pistols were to be produced in Austria; Glock, Inc. would be the U.S. importer and distributor.

Glock, Inc. issued its first news release on 1 December 1985, announcing that the Glock was here and available in its commercial version. In the second quarter of 1990, Glock built a new plant at the Smyrna, Georgia, location, which was expected to greatly expand the ability to handle increased sales. All pistols are still built in Austria, but now final assembly, quality control, and test-firing take place in Georgia.

I spoke with Bob Gates, national sales manager, a few

months after the new facility was operational. He told me that they'd expected it would take three or four years for the plant to reach 50-percent capacity, but that almost as soon as the facility came on line it was operating at 80-percent capacity due to the enormous increase in sales volume.

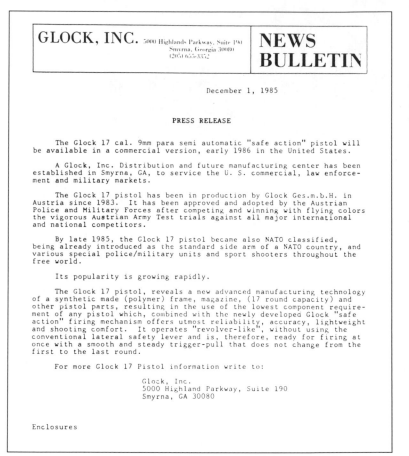

GLOCK, INC. 5000 Highlands Parkway, Suite 190
Smyrna, Georgia 30080
(205) 655-3352

NEWS BULLETIN

December 1, 1985

PRESS RELEASE

The Glock 17 cal. 9mm para semi automatic "safe action" pistol will be available in a commercial version, early 1986 in the United States.

A Glock, Inc. Distribution and future manufacturing center has been established in Smyrna, GA, to service the U. S. commercial, law enforcement and military markets.

The Glock 17 pistol has been in production by Glock Ges.m.b.H. in Austria since 1983. It has been approved and adopted by the Austrian Police and Military Forces after competing and winning with flying colors the vigorous Austrian Army Test trials against all major international and national competitors.

By late 1985, the Glock 17 pistol became also NATO classified, being already introduced as the standard side arm of a NATO country, and various special police/military units and sport shooters throughout the free world.

Its popularity is growing rapidly.

The Glock 17 pistol, reveals a new advanced manufacturing technology of a synthetic made (polymer) frame, magazine, (17 round capacity) and other pistol parts, resulting in the use of the lowest component requirement of any pistol which, combined with the newly developed Glock "safe action" firing mechanism offers utmost reliability, accuracy, lightweight and shooting comfort. It operates "revolver-like", without using the conventional lateral safety lever and is, therefore, ready for firing at once with a smooth and steady trigger-pull that does not change from the first to the last round.

For more Glock 17 Pistol information write to:

Glock, Inc.
5000 Highland Parkway, Suite 190
Smyrna, GA 30080

Enclosures

Glock Inc.'s first news release.

Gaston Glock demonstrating a fieldstripped Model 17 to Pete Dickey, technical editor of American Rifleman magazine. Note the pistol's slide in Mr. Glock's left hand. On the table in front of Glock are two empty magazines and a magazine loader, and in front of Mr. Dickey, another Model 17 with its magazine removed. (Photo courtesy of Randy Lamson of the National Rifle Association.)

In October 1990, Miami police officer Armando Valdes competed in the 1990 World Shoot IX Championships in Adelaide, South Australia, shooting an unaltered Glock Model 17L, serial number DA 017 US. He won the twenty-nine-course, nine-day event, Stock Class. He fired 300 rounds of Remington 130-gr. FMJ ammunition at distances ranging from 5 to 35 meters. Out of 21 Master Class competitors in the Stock Class, Valdes finished eleven percentage points ahead of the second-place shooter. Altogether, there were 306 Master Class competitors from all over the world competing, and in the Unlimited Class, Valdes' total scores ranked him in the top 12 percent, at forty-ninth place overall.

Glock and Dickey examine a disassembled Model 17. (Photo courtesy of Randy Lamson of the National Rifle Association.)

By the end of 1990 there were more than 300,000 Glock pistols in use throughout North America. By April 1991, more than 3,500 federal, state, and local law enforcement agencies had issued or authorized Glock pistols for duty use, and there were 200,000 pistols in the hands of law enforcement personnel alone.

Armando Valdes with his Model 17L and the first-place trophy he won in the 1990 World Shoot IX Championships in Adelaide, South Australia.

CHAPTER 2

The Media Fiasco

wo days after the 13 January 1985 opening of Glock's Smyrna, Georgia, facility, a Jack Anderson article appeared in the *Washington Post* entitled, "Qaddafi Buying Austrian Plastic Pistol." The article was picked up by UPI and, within days, appeared in numerous American and international newspapers. In typical form for Anderson and the news media, the original article and most of those subsequently published were filled with errors. The Glock instantly became known as the "hijacker special," the "invisible weapon," the "terrorist special," the "gun that defeats airport security," the "gun that can pass undetected through airport X-ray machines," and on and on, ad nauseam.

The Libyan Allegations

Prior to publication of his article, Anderson telephoned Glock. It mattered not one whit that the factory spokesperson told him Glock had never sold anything, directly or indirectly, to Libya. Glock also told Anderson no Libyan had ever contacted anyone there inquiring about a gun purchase, and no Glock personnel had ever gone to Libya. These and other denials of past, present, or contemplated future business with Libya failed to dissuade Anderson from publishing this and other allegations in his article, even though he knew they were untrue.

JACK ANDERSON and DALE VAN ATTA

Qaddafi Buying Austrian Plastic Pistols

Libyan dictator Muammar Qaddafi is in the process of buying more than 100 plastic handguns that would be difficult for airport security forces to detect.

Incredibly, the pistols are made in Austria—where Qaddafi-supported terrorists shot up the Vienna airport during Christmas week.

"This is crazy," one top official told us. "To let a madman like Qaddafi have access to such a pistol! Once it is in his hands, he'll give it to terrorists throughout the Middle East."

The handgun in question is the Glock 17, a 9mm pistol invented and manufactured by Gaston Glock in the village of Deutsch-Wagram, just outside Vienna. It is accurate, reliable and made almost entirely of hardened plastic. Only the barrel, slide and one spring are metal. Dismantled, it is frighteningly easy to smuggle past airport security.

In fact, one Pentagon security expert decided to demonstrate just how easy it would be to sneak a Glock 17 aboard an airliner. He stripped the gun down and disguised the metal parts in his carry-on luggage. For example, he wrapped the spring around a pair of eyeglasses.

The Pentagon man tested his system twice at Washington National Airport, and got past the security checks both times. He subsequently alerted airport security personnel, and taught them how to spot the elements of the pistol. Security measures have been tightened.

Intelligence sources tell us Qaddafi has nearly completed a deal to buy more than 100 Glock 17s, possibly as many as 300. They explain that Austrian arms merchants hoping to sell Qaddafi big-ticket items—such as tanks—are using the Glock 17s as "sweeteners" for future transactions.

A marketing official for Glock in Austria assured us that the company has not sold Libya any of the guns, at least not yet. He offered no information on current negotiations.

Austria's past dealings with Qaddafi suggest that even the obvious danger of such a sale would not be enough to bring government intervention. It was the first European country in nine years to entertain Qaddafi on an official state visit, in 1982. He used the platform provided by the Austrians in Vienna to denounce President Reagan.

The Austrians were rewarded for their attitude toward Arab extremists in 1981 when Palestinian terrorists assassinated Heinz Nittel, a prominent Austrian Jew and close friend of then-Chancellor Bruno Kreisky.

When Kreisky complained to Palestine Liberation Organization Chairman Yasser Arafat, the latter pointed the finger at his rival, Abu Nidal, and even offered to send a pair of "antiterrorist specialists" to Vienna to assist Austrian police. But Mossad, the Israeli secret service, learned that the two Palestinians had actually been sent to assassinate Egyptian President Anwar Sadat in Vienna, and to kill Kreisky, too, if he got in the way.

Austrian authorities arrested the two Palestinians at the Vienna airport, and found sharpshooters' weapons and grenades in their luggage. Follow-up searches of PLO safe houses in Austria turned up maps and plans for the Sadat assassination. The two gunmen were packed off to Beirut. Once again, Abu Nidal was blamed.

Jack Anderson's inflammatory article in the Washington Post *in January 1985 brought about a barrage of negative publicity for the Glock.*

On 22 January 1985, Gaston Glock issued a news release denying Anderson's claims and the media reports. But it was too late; Anderson's erroneous and defamatory publication had done widespread and profound damage.

Restoring Glock in the public eye was no simple task.

As part of his 16 May 1986 testimony before the U.S. House of Representatives Committee on the Judiciary, Subcommittee on Crime, Glock Vice President Karl F. Walter stated: "Glock has at no time since its foundation in 1963 offered directly or indirectly, or negotiated about, or concluded any deal, [for the sale of Glock firearms] to or with Libya, Libyan agents, or representatives or other individuals or entities representing Libya."

Austrian export regulations for firearms are quite rigid; the law requires prior issuance of export permits for each individual instance of firearms exportation, regardless of destination. High government officials from four Austrian ministries meet weekly to check each application before an export license can be approved. As verified in his letter of 23 April 1986, Karl Blecha, the Austrian minister of interior, confirmed that neither Glock nor any other individual, company, or entity representing Glock had ever applied for an export permit to Libya.

From the beginning, Glock has had self-imposed exportation restrictions even more stringent than those required by Austrian law. For example, for all export destinations other than Europe, the United States, and Canada, Glock allows shipment only when official end-user certificates are issued. Additionally, all export shipments of more than one hundred pistols must be to end-user authorities that are personally known to Glock Ges. m.b.H.

But Glock diligence doesn't stop there. In addition to all of the above, Glock restricts importers to their home territory, the only exceptions being upon prior agreement. Glock views transgressions as serious breaches of agency agreement and considers such grounds for cancellation of the agreement.

No importer has ever asked for, nor has Glock granted, permission to sell or ship to Libya. Glock states unequivocally that it "simply would not accept orders from Libya." No evidence has ever been presented demonstrating that even a single Glock firearm has appeared in Libya.

"Terrorist Pistol" Allegations

Austrian Ministry of Interior approval of the Glock Model 17 for production and commercial sale in 1982 signified that the gun had passed many tests and was determined to be no danger to the public safety. Among the many tests done by high-ranking Austrian security authorities were detectability tests conducted at the Vienna International Airport. It was concluded that Austrian airport security equipment and personnel could readily and clearly detect all individual components of the Glock 17 pistol. In a 23 April 1986 letter to Gaston Glock, Austrian Minister of Interior Blecha said: "In the course of our extensive testing of the GLOCK 17 and before it was approved and adopted, a number of general and airport security tests were performed. We may state that due to our experience the GLOCK 17 is detectable by airport security equipment in the same way as any other conventional pistol or revolver, standard alertness/training of security staff and proper setting of equipment provided."

On 12-14 February 1986, Glock, Riedl, and Walter met with four different federal agencies in Washington, D.C. The main purpose of these meetings was to determine exactly how U.S. airport security, and airport security in general, stacked up against Viennese airport security. All four of the visited federal agencies, including the Federal Aviation Administration (FAA), had tested the Glock 17 pistol and stated that it was readily detectable provided that security personnel are alert and diligently follow security guidelines.

On 14 February 1986, Glock, Riedl, and Walter met with U.S. government personnel at the Pentagon. Prior to this meeting, a DOD officer went to Austria to visit with Glock Ges. m.b.H. people, as well as Viennese International Airport security authorities. This officer's mission was to learn about European airport security methods and to report his findings back to the secretary of defense. During the Pentagon meeting, in the presence of, among others, the under secretary of counterterrorism, the under secretary of trade and security policy, and various Pentagon officials, this DOD officer reported that the Vienna Airport security is among Europe's finest.

Also during the meeting, Noel Koch, the under secretary of counterterrorism, revealed that it was he who was mentioned in Jack Anderson's 13 January *Washington Post* article as having "smuggled" a Glock Model 17 through Washington National Airport security checkpoints. He reported that he had partially disassembled the Model 17 and disguised some of the parts in various ways to evade detection.

Significantly, the under secretary also revealed that the Glock wasn't the only pistol he'd "smuggled" through Washington National Airport security on that occasion. A Heckler & Koch Model P-9 pistol that he'd taped, fully assembled, into his briefcase also sailed right through the security checkpoints. The Heckler & Koch Model P-9 is made entirely of metal and weighs 928 grams, over 43 percent more than a Glock Model 17 (the P-9 contains over 69 percent more metal by weight than the Model 17).

In the Pentagon meeting discussions, it was commonly understood that the fact that both the Glock and Heckler & Koch pistols had passed undetected through airport security checkpoints clearly indicated that the problem lay not with the Glock pistol, nor even with both pistols. Rather, the problem was one of insufficient alertness and training of security personnel and/or sensitivity of X-ray devices.

A quote from Walter's 15 May 1986 testimony before the U.S. House of Representatives Committee on the Judiciary, Subcommittee on Crime sums it up well:

> It was clearly pointed out [at the Pentagon meeting] that disclosure of the true test findings

could encourage mad people to test security with their guns and that this would not be in anyone's best interest; hence, no supplemental reports have been made to the media by the Pentagon Officials [sic] concerning the assembled H&K P-9 pistol in the Under Secretary's briefcase, which is approximately the same size [dimensionally] as the Glock 17 pistol that evaded security personnel as well.

Media-Fueled Legislative Hysteria

As is so frequently the case with matters such as these, the media lit a small fire, then poured fuel on it and fanned the flames until it became a raging inferno. And as they usually do in such situations, opportunistic legislators attempted to make political hay in the firelight.

It was widely suggested that the Glock pistol be banned. One of the chief proponents of such a ban was Representative Mario Biaggi from the 19th District in New York, who introduced a bill (HR 4223) proposing to ban the Glock Model 17. Benjamin Ward, the police commissioner of New York City, urged that Glock pistols be banned there. Among newspapers, the *Washington Post* led the pack espousing a ban of Glock pistols.

It is interesting to note that Commissioner Ward was discovered to carry a Glock Model 17 as his personal weapon for protection while, among other things, jogging in Central Park. The *Washington Post* ran articles praising the "state-of-the-art" Glock Model 17 pistol when police in Washington, D.C., selected it as their official duty sidearm. The Honorable Mario Biaggi never changed his public position about Glock pistols, but it is safe to assume that while serving prison time for taking bribes (subsequent to introduction of HR 4223), he had plenty of time to contemplate it.

The Media Fiasco

Anderson Undeterred by Truth

Despite the facts, Anderson published yet another article in the *Washington Post*, this time on 18 April 1986. In it he referred to a report by an unnamed West German "high-level official" (it is a common tactic of the American news media and other antigun people to quote unnamed sources) who tested the Glock Model 17 at the Stuttgart Airport. In his article, Anderson falsely stated that the completely assembled Glock Model 17 was "extremely hard to recognize on the X-ray screen. Disassembled, the weapon was x-rayed together with a camera in a camera bag. In this condition only the barrel could be detected as a thick black line. The plastic parts could not be detected."

But why should one expect Jack Anderson to heed the truth?

The respected German publication *Der Spiegel*, in an article about explosives and older X-ray equipment, reported a very different version of the same incident:

> American experts are talking of the "Ideal Weapon for Hi-Jackers." The *Washington Post* reported promptly that Libya's Qaddafi has already bought 100 pieces. The U.S. television frightened the nation with a test report: In the International Airport in Washington, a reporter was able to smuggle the plastic shooting instrument through security gates.
>
> Safety authorities in German airports like the Hannover Airport state that the U.S. discussion is "amusing."
>
> For some time training has been conducted with weapons containing synthetic material.
>
> The Hannover Airport can identify easily toy pistols.
>
> That the Glock 17 is easily detectable was

tested by the police arms expert, Siegfreid Huebner, at the Stuttgart Airport. He disassembled the pistol and concealed parts in a camera case between flashlight and films/camera.

On two safety controls, which are equipped with the modern X-ray unit High Scan 9050, the Stuttgart arms expert got caught—next to the metal pieces, plastic parts were clearly recognized.

Following Anderson's 15 January 1986 article, *The Kansas City Star* (7 April 1986) quoted Billie H. Vincent, director of civil aviation security for the FAA: "Contrary to the information that is being put out now . . . the Glock 17 is detectable on all of our airport systems, whether it is the metal detector or the X-ray system. The handgun, even the plastic grip, is detectable on the X-ray system at the airport."

The same article stated that "federal officials dispute Mr. Anderson's account. Mr. Vincent, in congressional testimony, said he was present and the Glock 17 was visible on the X-ray screen. 'Any failure to detect that weapon is operator error,' he said."

Varied Reaction to Media Campaign

The Austrian trade commissioner in New York received the following anonymous letter in March 1986:

> Sirs:
> It is not difficult to understand how Austria would be capable of this ultimate desecration of values and, ultimately, of life, by permitting the manufacture and exportation of a blatant hijacker's weapon, made of plastic. One has to recall Austria's joining forces with Hitler as a most eager & willing ally, then disclaiming responsibility. This to avoid costly reparations.

Then there was the spiking of wine with antifreeze. What more can you expect from a nation of whores, whose only claim to fame is a nostalgic waltz, a reminiscence on Empire and a supersaturated Catholicism to redeem them from their present iniquities.

This letter to the editor appeared in the 6 February 1986 issue of the *New York Times*:

The pioneer manufacturer of the plastic handgun is the Austrian company of Gaston Glock, near Vienna. The Glock 17 is a 9-millimeter pistol, composed almost entirely of plastic. Only the barrel, slide and one spring are of metal. Broken down, these few metal parts could be hidden innocuously to escape X-ray detection. Col. Muammar el-Qaddafi is reportedly in the process of completing a deal to buy at least 100 of the plastic guns.

In its "Inside the Beltway" column of 7 March 1986, the *Washington Times* stated that ". . . the Austrian Glock 17 . . . can be smuggled past metal detectors."

An article in the 28 April 1986 issue of *Fortune* stated that "The Glock 17 pistol is the latest terrorist weapon to menace air travelers around the world." The article republished most of Anderson's lies about the Glock 17 and airport security X-ray devices, but went on to state: "The weakest link in airport security remains the inspectors, who get bored and overlook suspicious objects."

Composite Materials in Firearms

Synthetic and/or composite materials have been used in small arms for at least half a century. During World War II, the German MP-40, FG-42, and G-41 weapons used lower receivers, pistol grips, and handguards of synthetic and/or composite materials. The H&K Model VP70Z, a 9mm Parabellum pistol, had a plastic receiver.

In recent times numerous U.S.-manufactured (military and private sector) firearms have begun to use synthetic and/or composite components for some, but not all of their component parts. The M14, M16/AR-15, Colt Sporter, and their myriad clones utilize synthetics and/or composites extensively; the High Standard Model 10 shotgun's stock and receiver were made from composite material; the Winchester Model 50 shotgun (produced from 1954 to 1961) had a composite barrel; the Remngton Nylon 66 .22-caliber rifle was made from synthetics; and so on.

Small arms substantially (though not entirely) constructed from synthetic and/or composite materials are quite common today. There are at least hundreds of thousands in the United States private sector, and virtually millions in use by militaries throughout the world.

As Walter stated in his congressional testimony, "A handgun made entirely of composite materials that will meet military or law enforcement criteria or sporting needs is not commonly or publicly available and/or is classified."

• • • • •

Unquestionably, Glock pistols are detectable at properly operated and correctly calibrated airport and other similar security checkpoints. As the *Kansas City Star* article mentioned earlier in this chapter stated, ". . . the Bureau of Alcohol, Tobacco and Firearms . . . issue[d] a special memorandum to its regional offices, according to information obtained by the *Kansas City Star* under a Freedom of Information Act request. The unsigned memo said the Glock 17 is a 'high-tech, high-quality firearm and its use of plastic gives it an advantage in being light-weight—not in concealability.'"

Although Jack Anderson seems to have lost interest in disseminating lies and distortions about Glock pistols, the news media rarely miss an opportunity. For example, on 17 October 1991, in Killeen, Texas, George Hennard killed twenty-three people in a cafeteria. Electronic and print news media nationwide had a field day reporting that Hennard used a Glock pistol. What some of them failed to report, however, is that he also used a Ruger P-89. Indeed, he fired 61 rounds from the Ruger and only 41 rounds from the Glock. All magazines for the Ruger were empty, and the pistol was found with its slide locked open; all 28 unfired rounds were found in Glock magazines.

The *Los Angeles Times* ran a three-page piece mentioning the Glock numerous times, including a sidebar discussing the selective-fire Model 18, but said nary a word about the Ruger. A sorely misinformed writer named Tom Goff wrote that the Glock 17 was so named because that's how many rounds it holds. But perhaps the most egregious of all was a cartoon that appeared in the *Bay Guardian* in San Francisco. It depicts three executive types around a boardroom table beneath a banner reading, "In the House of Glock Handguns . . ." The caption reads, "Think of it this way . . . One of our own customers stages a dramatic products demonstration. It doesn't cost us a cent. Overnight Glock is a household word. Things could be worse, gents. Colt or Remington or Smith & Wesson could have gotten all the publicity. It's a victory for the little guy."

CHAPTER 3

The Law Enforcement Phenomenon

evolvers have been the sidearm of choice for U.S. police throughout most of the nation's history. It wasn't until late 1954, when Smith & Wesson sent prototypes of its Models 39 and 44 to law enforcement for evaluation, that anyone seriously attempted to unseat the wheelgun. Even then, it took about fifteen years until a few law enforcement agencies began to realize the revolver had become inadequate. In the late 1960s, the Illinois State Police adopted the Smith & Wesson Model 39, and slowly others began to follow suit.

Smith & Wesson Model 19, a typical police-type revolver.

By the end of 1990, half the nation's state police departments had switched to semiautomatics, to say nothing of countless federal agencies and local departments. As of this writing, 3,500 federal, state, and local agencies and departments had adopted or authorized the Glock for duty use, and there were about 220,000 in use by American law enforcement personnel.

Beretta M9, the current official sidearm of the U.S. military.

When the U.S. military selected Beretta's M9 (military version of the Model 92F) as its official sidearm in the early 1980s, many law enforcement agencies followed suit. Around the same time, Smith & Wesson's Second-Generation semiautos were introduced and began making inroads into law enforcement. S&W's Third Generation came on the scene in 1989, bringing the company continued success in selling to police customers.

But by that time something had happened that would soon astonish the firearms and law enforcement communities. Glock had arrived, and those worlds would never again be the same.

Glock Police Sales Begin

In March 1986 the first sale of Glock pistols to U.S. law enforcement was made to the two-person Colby, Kansas, Police Department. Next came a sale to the somewhat (but not very much) larger sheriff's department in Flagler County, Florida, and the phenomenon had begun.

St. Paul, Minnesota, was the first big-city police department to adopt the Glock (first the Model 17; later the Model 19) as its official duty weapon, but the "really big" law enforcement happening was yet to come.

It began following a controversial officer-involved shooting in 1982. Chief Clarence Dickson of the Miami Police Department, worried about departmental liability, decreed that all service revolvers must be converted to double-action-only, a common tactic of many police departments, including the liability-prone Los Angeles PD. But by the mid-1980s many police groups were pressing their administrations for more state-of-the-art duty weapons.

By 1986, Miami police officers, like so many others around the country, were lobbying for semiautos that would make their tactical capabilities at least competitive with what they were facing on the street. Chief Dickson, ever mindful of liability exposure, said he'd authorize what they wanted if they could come up with a high-capacity 9mm pistol that was double-action-only.

Miami PD tried Beretta, SIG-Sauer, and Smith & Wesson. None had a double-action-only pistol, and none was interested in producing one to suit Miami's needs. A representative (anonymous by request) of one, however, suggested that Miami contact Glock. No one at Miami PD had ever heard of Glock, but in the fall of 1986, Sergeant Paul Palank, chief firearms instructor for Miami PD, contacted Karl Walter at Glock, Inc. One thing led to another, and in May 1987 Miami PD began a pilot program wherein twenty-five officers began testing and utilizing Glock Model 17 pistols. One test included throwing and dropping a loaded (primed case only) Model 17 numerous times on steel and concrete from distances of up to 60 feet. Another fully loaded (with real ammunition) Model 17 was submerged in saltwater for fifty hours, then retrieved and discharged; it fired flawlessly. Then the same pistol was reloaded and left exposed to the air for two days but, upon firing, malfunctioned after the first round fired. Upon inspection it was determined that some corrosion had formed inside the weapon that had interfered with slide cycling. The pistol was unloaded, swished in a bucket of kerosene, and reloaded; it then fired flawlessly. One of Miami's final tests of the Glock 17 was to fire 1,000 rounds of Winchester Silvertip ammunition in forty-five minutes; all rounds were fired with no malfunctions.

In the fall of 1987 the Miami Police Department became the first "really big" law enforcement agency in the United States to adopt the Glock pistol, initially purchasing 1,300 Model 17s.

Resistance

But all did not go smoothly for Glock in law enforcement sales after that. Many police administrators, trainers, and other personnel are traditionalists and, in many cases, can be very stubborn. As the eighties came to an end, many police traditionalists had seen the writing on the wall and had grudgingly accepted the fact that semiautos were here to stay. But many of those same people adamantly opposed Glock pistols.

The most common criticism centered around the

Glock pistol's lack of an affirmative safety device—one requiring some cognitive action before firing capability is achieved.

On the other hand, it is often argued that police-type revolvers have no external safety device, affirmative or otherwise, and there's never been a problem there. A more sophisticated version of that argument holds that many high-tech semiautos equipped with decocking levers also have no external safety device, and there seems to be no problem there, either.

Opponents of the Glock counter with the argument that while it is true that police-type revolvers have no external safeties, they do have long, hard trigger forces that make such safeties (virtually) unnecessary. The same applies to modern pistols equipped with decocking levers, at least for the first shot. But Glock pistols, the argument runs, have shorter trigger travel and far less required force, thus rendering them unsafe without some sort of affirmative safety device.

Original Glock Triggers

At first all Glock pistols were shipped with trigger connectors that required 5 pounds of force to actuate. Then the Metro Dade Police Department (whose jurisdiction covers much of the metropolitan area in and around the eastern and coastal areas of the county not covered by Miami PD) wanted greater trigger force, so Glock changed the 90-degree angle of the connector ramp to 105 degrees for them so that 8 pounds of force was required to actuate the trigger; the initial order was for 1,200 units. Soon, 8-pound connectors were shipped on most law enforcement orders. It helped, but some were still unsatisfied.

Glock pistol triggers were designed to have light pressure requirements for the first portion of rearward travel, which is considerably farther than the second, and final, portion of travel. In the original design, the initial trigger travel phase was resisted only by a very light coil-type spring. The second phase began when the rear extension of the trigger bar contacted the angled ramp of the connector. Pressure required to move the trigger rearward during the second phase was considerably higher; forces of the coil-type trigger spring and the friction necessary to move the trigger bar extension down the angled ramp combined to 5 pounds for the "standard" connector and 8 pounds for the "police" connector. Glock also offered a 3.5-pound connector for Model 17L competition pistols only.

A standard 5-pound connector.

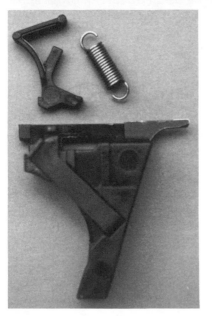

Trigger mechanism housing with connector in place and another connector alongside, oriented to correspond to the one installed on the housing. Muzzle direction is to the right, as indicated by the direction of the ejector, located at the upper right of the housing. Shown directly above, oriented as they would be if installed in the housing, are a New York trigger and a coil-type trigger spring.

Enter the New York Trigger Spring

Near the beginning of 1990, Glock introduced a replacement for the original coil-type trigger spring. Developed for a county law enforcement department in New York, it was actually first used by the New York State Police. It is officially known as the "New York trigger spring" but is often called simply the "New York trigger."

The original coil-type trigger spring hooks on one end to the trigger mechanism housing and on the other to the bottom of the cruciform portion of the so-called sear plate, which is part of the trigger bar. The New York trigger—a strangely shaped part made mostly from polymer, with a small, flat piece of spring steel affixed—press-fits down inside of the trigger mechanism housing and pushes upward on the underside (at the rear) of the sear plate's cruciform portion, but does not actually attach to it as does the coil-type trigger spring.

The New York trigger spring's main purpose is to alter trigger "feel" to more closely resemble that of a police-type revolver. To some extent it does that, although it cannot be said that a Glock pistol with a New York trigger spring installed "feels like" a double-action revolver.

Equipped with a New York trigger spring, a Glock pistol's trigger still has two stages, but there is more and different resistance during the initial phase. And in the second phase, there is an increase in required trigger force.

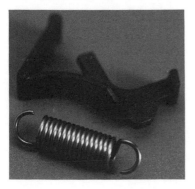

A New York trigger spring (top) and a standard coil-type trigger spring (bottom).

33

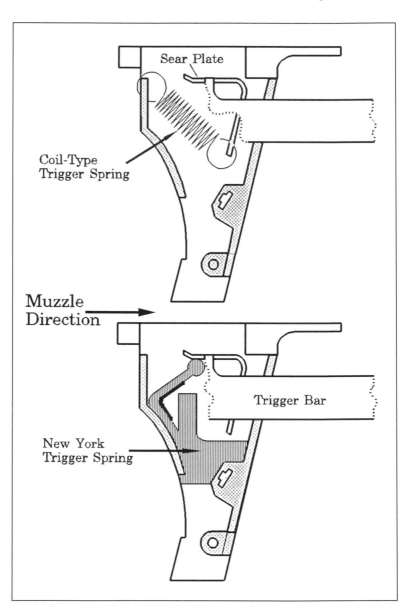

Sear Plate

Coil-Type
Trigger Spring

Muzzle
Direction

Trigger Bar

New York
Trigger Spring

Comparison of a coil-type trigger spring and a New York trigger spring, both installed.

There are actually two New York trigger springs. The "standard" adds 2.5 to 3.5 pounds of required trigger force, and the "+" adds 4 to 6 pounds of required trigger force. Combined with a 5-pound connector, total required trigger force is 7.5 to 8.5 pounds for the "standard" and 9 to 11 pounds for the "+" New York trigger spring.

New York Trigger Spring Caveat

Glock is adamant that New York trigger springs be installed *only* in combination with 5-pound connectors. Due to the geometry of the 105-degree angled ramp on the 8-pound connector and the magnitude of the force vectors induced by the "+" New York trigger spring, the two combined in the same pistol can cause problems. In my opinion, it is a serious mistake to combine the two.

(In that regard I must come to the defense of my friend and colleague, Massad Ayoob. In his extraordinary pair of articles on Glocks in the September 1990 issue of *Guns* magazine, he mentioned that his personal Glock 19 is equipped with a New York trigger spring and an 8-pound connector. When he wrote that, and even later when it was published, Glock had not announced that New York trigger springs should be used only with 5-pound connectors. At the time of this writing, he advised that he had swapped the 8-pound connector for a 5-pounder upon learning of Glock's admonition.)

Are Glocks Unsafe?

Some people maintain that even with 8-pound connectors or with New York trigger springs installed, Glock pistols are unsafe because they lack an affirmative safety device.

There are generally two arguments made to support this position: 1) without an affirmative safety, Glock pistols can be taken from their owners and used on them; and 2) "accidental" discharges during reholstering attempts or when in the hands of children would be all but eliminated if an affirmative safety were installed.

Disarming

As for disarming, it is an incontrovertible fact that the overwhelming percentage of those disarmed by criminals have their own guns turned on them, regardless of the type of revolver or pistol they are carrying. This has remained constant for decades, since the days when revolvers were nearly ubiquitous in law enforcement. Charles Remsberg, author of *Street Survival*, one of the best books ever written on police procedures and tactics, wrote: "A notoriously high percentage—some estimates say 90 percent—of suspects who succeed in disarming police officers end up attempting to kill them [with their own guns]." In addition, 25 percent of all police officers shot in the line of duty are shot with their own guns, and another 10 percent with another officer's gun. However, suggesting that an affirmative safety on a gun is an answer to this problem is avoiding the issue.

Ed Davis, former Chief of Police of the Los Angeles PD, argued against upgrading his department's .38 Special revolvers to .357 Magnums, saying, "In any given year x percent of my personnel will be shot with their own weapons. I would rather have them shot with a .38 than a .357."

The issue is not that guns must be made difficult to actuate, or that cops should be equipped with less powerful guns, which would only put them at a severe disadvantage in their jobs and unreasonably endanger their lives. It would be far better to address the problem of why their guns are taken away so easily and frequently. If more cops were provided with weapon-retention training, the percentage of cops shot with their own guns would plummet. It seems far more sensible to equip them with effective weapon-retention skills than with inferior and less effective weapons.

Between January 1975 and June 1976, nine Kansas City, Missouri, police officers were disarmed. The KCPD planning unit conducted a study to determine why their cops were being disarmed and what could be done to stop it. The research revealed the lack of any system of techniques or training to effectively counter disarmament attempts.

As a result, James Lindell, physical training supervisor for KCPD's Regional Police Academy, developed what was then known as his Revolver Retention System. It was instituted in August 1976. A survey taken over the fifty-two-month period following implementation revealed that no police officer trained in the Lindell Method was disarmed, although several who had not received training were. Since that time the Lindell Method—evolved to its current Lindell Handgun/Long Gun Retention & Disarming System—has become the standard weapon- retention system among law enforcement agencies the world over.

Unfortunately, while many departments and agencies around the world provide training in Lindell's or some other system of weapon retention, not nearly enough do. There are far too many that provide no training whatsoever in weapon-retention awareness or techniques. It doesn't make sense to rely on a mechanical device that will keep a disarmed person from being shot with his or her own gun if and only if: 1) it was "on" before the disarming, 2) it didn't get "wiped" off during the disarming, 3) the criminal doesn't know how to take it off, 4) the criminal doesn't get lucky and figure it out or get it off by trial and error, or 5) it doesn't fail.

Regarding the third point, in arguing for an affirmative safety on Glock pistols in the September 1990 *Guns* articles, Ayoob asserted that "guns are made to be held with the finger on the trigger." As an instructor with three decades of experience in high-stress training where human factors are vital, I agree unequivocally with his observation. But I have another of my own: affirmative safeties are also designed to be ergonomically appropriate. So while it's true that one can imagine instances in which a criminal would be stopped or slowed down by an affirmative safety, it's also true that it doesn't take a genius to figure out how to flick one from "on" to "off."

"Accidental" Discharges

As for "accidental" discharges, consider the following. Surveys in 1989 and 1990 showed that more than 40 percent of law enforcement personnel switching to semi-autos acquired Glocks, but reports of "accidental" discharge problems exceeding what already existed with revolvers (as expected by some) did not materialize. Miami PD reported that "accidental" discharges dropped to less than half of what they were with revolvers in recent years before the transition.

In 1989 the Finnish police were interested in Glock pistols but were undecided about the affirmative safety question. In response, Glock sent them two versions: a standard production pistol and a prototype with a single additional part—a frame-mounted, lever-style affirmative safety on the left side of the receiver. After evaluation and testing, Finland decided against the affirmative safety and adopted the Glock in standard version. No one can argue with Glock's assertion (and that of many professional firearm trainers, including Jeff Cooper and myself) that the only truly reliable safety device isn't found on the gun. Every firearms manufacturer and responsible trainer cautions that mechanical safety devices must never be relied upon to assure that the gun won't go off.

Keeping the trigger finger off the trigger (except in certain severe tactical situations) until ready to fire will absolutely prevent a properly functioning modern pistol from discharging. That is indisputable, but the argument is whether or not admonitions and training are sufficient to keep people from pulling triggers negligently and/or unintentionally. (NOTE: As a full-time firearms instructor who is also trained in the law, I eschew the common phrase "accidental discharge," because the word "accidental" implies that no one was at fault, and some of us believe that can never be true where firearms are concerned. Instead, I use the term "negligent discharge," because when a gun goes off unintentionally it is always due to someone's negligence.)

Suggesting that Glock's lack of an affirmative safety causes "accidental" discharges, Ayoob cited nine actual cases:

1. A Miami suspect is killed after slamming his head back into the muzzle of the arresting officer's Glock.
2. A Jacksonville, Florida, suspect is killed after the arresting officer's Glock discharges while the officer is attempting to handcuff him.
3. A two-year-old child kills herself after finding the loaded Glock her Washington, D.C., police officer father placed on the bed.
4. During a confrontation immediately following a high-speed chase, a California Highway Patrol (CHP) officer unintentionally discharges his Glock into the suspect's head, killing him.
5. A Dallas, Texas, police officer shoots himself in the leg on the department range while attempting to reholster his Glock with his finger on the trigger.
6. A DEA agent shoots himself in the ass while trying to shove his Glock into his waistband during a raid.
7. A Miami police officer discharges his Glock while attempting to holster it with his finger on the trigger.
8. A Coral Gables, Florida, police officer discharges his Glock while attempting to holster it with his finger on the trigger.
9. A U.S. Marshall on an aircraft discharges a loaded Glock into his lower body while shoving it into his waistband.

In reviewing those cases, I was reminded of something that happened in the 1960s. More than twenty-five years ago, Boeing introduced its Model 727. Not long after adoption by several airlines, the three-engine jet with a (then) highly sophisticated swept wing, T-tail, and other high-tech design features experienced a disturbing series of crashes. The news media, followed naturally by several legislators, began a hysterical campaign decrying the B-727, which resulted in serious overreaction and unfortunate and unnecessary anguish among the general public.

Following the tragic crash of a United Airlines B-727 on approach to the Salt Lake City airport, United and other airlines discovered an interesting and revealing fact: all of the flight crews on 727s that had crashed had been relatively inexperienced on swept-wing jets, despite having had considerable experience on straight-wing, propeller-driven airliners. It was noted that there were considerable differences in the flying characteristics of the two types of aircraft, and that there might be some connection between this fact and the crashes.

Instead of prematurely condemning the airplane as unsafe because several had crashed, the investigators remained objective and were able to determine that it was more likely some factor other than a design defect in the Boeing tri-jet that was causing the crashes. Soon it was concluded that pilot error seemed to have caused each of the crashes.

Boeing and the airlines that then owned 727s revamped their training programs. Pilots were retrained, and those newly transitioning to the modern craft were afforded considerably more initial training focused on the differences between the old equipment they were leaving behind and the new, state-of-the-art equipment to which they were switching. Virtually overnight, crash levels dropped to far lower than before, even lower than with the old prop liners.

Around the same period, the hot new corporate jet designed and originally built by Bill Lear was taking the aviation world by storm. But suddenly tragedy struck, much like it had so recently with the airlines and their Boeing 727s. Learjets seemed to be crashing left and right.

As with the Boeings, it was discovered that pilots who had first seemed experienced and qualified were actually inadequately trained to handle the little plane with its sophisticated fighterlike performance. Despite years of experience and thousands of hours in the air, the newly certified Lear pilots were getting into trouble. Gates Tire Company, the new owner of Learjet, contracted with American Airlines to train Lear pilots; as in the case of the B-727, Lear crashes decreased dramatically, virtually overnight.

Today the Boeing 727 is one of the most widely used airliners in the world—and one of the safest. Likewise, Learjets are among the most ubiquitous and well-known of all corporate jets and have a safety record that is among the best.

So what can we in the firearms community learn from the experiences of the aviation community? I speak from experience when I say that today's Glock safety concerns and those surrounding the Boeing 727 and Lear Model 23 in the sixties are astonishingly similar. I first attended Jet Commander school in 1964 and, in 1967, became the youngest captain ever certified in the four-engine Lockheed JetStar. Before leaving aviation after more than twenty years to attend law school, I would be a flight instructor and training captain, as well as an FAA pilot and flight instructor examiner for all certificates up to and including airline transport pilots.

Similarly, after thirty years of job-related and personal experience with firearms, I acquired my first Glock pistol in the same year Glock came to America. As a full-time firearms trainer, an NRA law enforcement firearms instructor, and a Glock Armorer and Glock Police Transition Instructor, I can state unequivocally that, as with those of the 727 and the Learjets in the sixties, the safety concerns surrounding the Glock are nonissues. In both instances, a high-tech, state-of-the-art device was blamed for safety-related tragedies when, in actuality, the problem lay not with the device at all but with inadequate training resulting in relatively few, but highly significant, "accidents."

In reviewing Ayoob's nine cases, I divided them into four categories, as follows:

1. The five law enforcement personnel injured—the Dallas, Miami, and Coral Gables police officers, the DEA agent, and the U.S. Marshall—all of whom discharged their Glocks during reholstering or waistband shove attempts.

2. The two suspects killed in Miami and Jacksonville during arrest and/or subdue attempts.

3. The child killed after finding her father's loaded Glock left out on the bed.

4. The suspect killed by a CHP officer following a high-speed chase.

Let's review the categorized cases to see if it can be clearly determined whether or not the Glock pistols common to them all—specifically the Glock's lack of an affirmative safety—was the cause.

Category 1: It's well known among professional firearms trainers that improper reholstering is a leading cause of "accidental" discharges. Such incidents have occurred for years, probably as long as people have been carrying handguns in holsters. An inept, distracted, or otherwise incompetent person capable of attempting to reholster a weapon with his or her finger on the trigger will also be insensitive or unaware enough that neither the type of gun nor the characteristics of its trigger will likely make any difference.

Another way of looking at it is that operating an affir-

42

mative safety before reholstering a pistol and keeping your finger off the trigger are both correctly classified as proper gun-handling procedures. So if an individual fails to adhere to proper gun-handling procedures by keeping his or her finger off the trigger, why expect him or her to adhere to proper gun-handling procedures by actuating an affirmative safety?

During a telephone conversation about these cases, Ayoob expressed concern that the Glock, more than most other handguns, is susceptible to unintentional discharge during reholstering if, after rolling around on the ground with a suspect, an officer attempts to reholster with a twig or some such thing in the holster that could catch the trigger and make the gun go off. "It's the only gun that I advocate looking at during reholstering, and how are you going to do that at night?" he said.

About the examples he cited in his *Guns* article, Ayoob said, "In all probability, none of these tragedies would have occurred if the pistol in question had been locked on 'safe' via a thumb latch." In the same conversation, he stood by this statement but admitted that the cited cases in this category could have happened with guns other than Glocks. It's his opinion, however, that such things are more likely with Glocks than with other guns.

I'm not certain Ayoob and I disagree that those unintentional discharges could have happened with any handgun but were more likely to happen with a Glock. No, I think it's more that we differ on the degree of likelihood. I tend to think it just as likely, or nearly so, that they could have happened with other guns as with Glocks; Massad thinks not.

As a pragmatist, and a legally trained one at that, I tend to view most things from a balancing perspective. We all agree that nothing's perfect, so the issue is, do the liabilities of Glock pistols' imperfections, however slight, outweigh the benefits of their superior design? Ayoob admittedly is very fond of his Glocks but is bothered by the things mentioned above. No one loves Glocks more than I, nor is anyone more liability conscious, yet I consider Glocks' significant advantages to far outweigh any so-called disadvantages.

In my opinion, blaming equipment for operator failures may be easy or desirable, but it isn't the right thing to do.

Category 2: What can one say about situations such as these? Properly maintained modern guns simply don't discharge from impact trauma. And of all pistols, Glocks underwent (and continue to undergo) the most rigorous possible impact trauma testing (usually called drop testing). Glock's ingenious drop safety design is virtually foolproof, but it's supplemented with an industry-standard firing-pin block, so discharge from impact trauma without the operator's finger on the trigger is impossible.

Furthermore, an affirmative safety is no guarantee that something similar to these examples won't happen. I'm reminded of a case I worked on while a clerk in law school: A private citizen carrying a licensed unmodified Colt Government Model got into an altercation and clubbed someone over the head several times with the pistol. The last time he struck the unfortunate adversary, the pistol discharged and the man died.

Remember, affirmative safeties (often unknowingly moved to the unsafe position) do not assure safety. The only thing you should ever bet your life (or someone else's) on is good gun handling resting on a firm foundation of solid training.

Category 3: The death of a child is always tragic; when the death is totally unnecessary, it's doubly heart-rending. Moreover, to professional firearms trainers and those knowledgeable in such matters, the death of a child that results from a gun owner's negligence is considered criminal. That the person responsible for the youngster's death is a grief-stricken parent is no reason to shift the blame elsewhere.

Who among us would load a pistol equipped with an affirmative safety, check that the safety was on, then point the gun at a child's head and pull the trigger? Anyone who would rely to such an unreasonable extent on a mechanical safety device should not have a gun. All too often a child has found a loaded gun and, despite safety devices, long, hard trigger pulls, and other things, has managed to innocently kill another child or himself.

Every person who owns a gun is absolutely responsible for everything that comes out of it. This is non-negotiable. There can be no excuses, no shirking of responsibility. If that Washington, D.C., police officer had placed some pistol other than a Glock on his bed and then left the room as he did, it's unknown if his little girl would be alive or dead now. What is certain, however, is that regardless of the type of gun he put there, such irresponsible behavior always has been and always will be inexcusable.

As a parent, it pained me profoundly to write the words in the three preceding paragraphs, but as a responsible gun owner and professional firearms trainer, it would be dishonest to temper them; the conclusions are unavoidable.

Category 4: There are two distinct elements in this case that must be addressed. First, the fact that the incident occurred immediately following a high-speed chase, and second, there was "contact" between the California Highway Patrol officer and the suspect.

It has long been known by law enforcement agencies that the potential for police abuse, including but not limited to excessive use of force, is extremely high immediately following high-speed chases. Many departments have regulations and procedures directly addressing such situations. Unfortunately, they do not always work, as demonstrated by the now infamous LAPD case wherein the brutal beating of Rodney King immediately after a high-speed chase was caught on videotape.

CHP officials refused to provide much information

about the incident cited by Ayoob because the case, which occurred in 1989 in the East Bay region of the San Francisco area, remained unresolved at the time of this writing. One firearms training officer did state, however, that the incident had no impact on the May 1990 CHP Academy's weapons training staff report entitled "Test and Evaluation: 10mm Semiautomatic Pistol," which was very unfavorable to Glock pistols.

As of this writing it is unknown specifically what happened other than that, as Ayoob reported, the CHP officer and the suspect made contact, and the gun fired unintentionally.

In recent years the California Highway Patrol has had more than its share of incidents involving excessive use of force, both with and without firearms. During those situations, officer constraint has often been sorely lacking. One such incident that occurred just a few miles from the location of the case Ayoob cited struck rather close to home for me: for no reason that ever became apparent, I was held at gunpoint for about twenty minutes by a CHP officer who repeatedly threatened to kill me. For most of that time he held his revolver to my head, and when it was pointed at my face I could tell that he was slowly squeezing and releasing the trigger because I was able to see the cylinder turn, then return as he relaxed trigger pressure.

For the record, he never alleged that I was wanted for anything, never even checked for wants or warrants, and continued threatening to kill me right up to the very moment he let me go. During the nearly one dozen court appearances following the incident, the California Highway Patrol vehemently resisted my "Pitchess Motion" (compelling an *in camera* review of the officer's personnel file to reveal any other excessive-use-of-force incidents in which he may have been involved), but reportedly reprimanded him and returned him to the academy for retraining.

The point about the case Ayoob mentioned in his article is that there was a shooting following a high-speed chase where the officer happened to be equipped with a Glock. Lacking any facts linking the pistol to the cause of the shooting, but knowing what we know about officers' behavioral tendencies following high-speed chases and CHP officers' recent history of excessive force, it seems patently unfair and unwarranted to blame the Glock in this case.

· · · · ·

As mentioned at the beginning of this chapter, by the spring of 1991 3,500 federal, state, and local law enforcement agencies and departments in the United States had adopted or approved Glock pistols for duty use. By then there were 220,000 Glock pistols in law enforcement hands.

In five short years, Glock has overcome considerable resistance in U.S. law enforcement circles. Its share of that market and its continuing growth rate (since November 1990, 800 departments and agencies have climbed on the Glock bandwagon) are astonishing—and absolutely unprecedented in the firearms community.

There will always be some for whom Glocks are not desirable, and that's okay. Reasonable minds can differ, and often do, even in law enforcement circles. An illustration of that notion can be found in the following chapter.

CHAPTER 4

The CHP and Scottsdale Reports

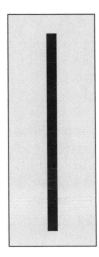

n September 1989 the California Highway Patrol Academy weapons staff rendered its "10mm Testing and Evaluation" report. The purpose was to evaluate and compare available 10mm ammunition with the 9mm, .45 ACP, .357 Magnum, and .38 +P+ then in use by the CHP.

The California Highway Patrol 10mm Testing and Evaluation Report

Five weapons were used in the testing:
1. Smith & Wesson Model 1006 10mm (prototype)
2. Smith & Wesson Model 4516 .45 ACP
3. Smith & Wesson Model 5906 9mm
4. Smith & Wesson Model 67 .38 Special
5. Smith & Wesson Model 686 .357 Magnum

Six types of ammunition were used in the testing:
1. Winchester 10mm 175-gr. Silvertip hollowpoint (STHP)
2. Federal 10mm 180-gr. jacketed hollowpoint (JHP), also known as the FBI Lite round
3. Federal .45 ACP 185-gr. STHP
4. Federal 9mm 115-gr. JHP
5. Federal .38 Special 110-gr. +P+ JHP
6. Remington .357 Magnum 125-gr. JHP

A series of four tests were conducted:

1. Chronotach tests to determine: a) velocity in feet per second and b) energy, using the formula of velocity squared times the quotient of the bullet weight in grains divided by 450,800 [V^2 x (bullet weight in grains/450,800)].
2. Penetration in ordnance gelatin to determine: a) expansion in thousandths of an inch and b) penetration in inches (8 to 12 inches considered optimum).
3. Recoil using videotaped CHP officers and cadets as subjects and recoil comparisons provided by Winchester based on a standard Sporting Arms and Ammunition Manufacturers Institute (SAAMI) formula.
4. Body armor penetration (10mm ammunition only).

The results of these tests (except the body armor penetration and recoil tests) are depicted by the chart that follows, which is reproduced directly from the CHP report.

Body armor penetration tests for the two 10mm rounds were conducted by firing each round into standard CHP issue PACA Type B body armor panels. One round each was fired into the panels that were placed over a block of ordnance gelatin. The Winchester STHP penetrated five layers of the first panel, and the Federal FBI Lite failed to penetrate even the first layer.

The CHP "10mm Testing and Evaluation" report's conclusion was as follows:

The performance of the Winchester 175-gr. round was excellent. It delivered over 530 pounds of energy, expanded to over .700 caliber and penetrated very well, over 15 inches. The recoil generated by this round, however, was very high, higher even than the Department's currently issued .357 Magnum round. Although the recoil was quite heavy, it was still manageable for some shooters and would be considered an excellent round for those who could manage it.

The Federal 180-gr. load, on the other hand, generated much less recoil than the Winchester 175 gr.-load. This, of course, made it much more manageable by all shooters. Even the smallest of shooters was able to fire the weapon and still maintain control. The muzzle energy levels generated were also quite a bit less than the 175-gr. Winchester at 308 foot pounds. Its expansion and penetration, however, were still comparable to the more powerful Winchester load. More importantly, this 10mm load, even in its more docile configuration, still delivers just as much energy as the Department's 9mm test round with more penetration and expansion.

California Highway Patrol Bullet Comparison Test

Test Bullet Caliber/Type	Ammunition Manufacturer	Weight Grains	Velocity fps	Depth inches	Expansion caliber	Muzzle Energy
9MM/JHP	Winchester[1]	115	1090	11.5	.625	303
10MM/STHP	Winchester	175	1170	15.25	.702	531
10MM/JHP	Federal[2]	180	879	16.5+	.701	308
.45 ACP/STHP	Winchester	185	953	13.5	.767	373
.38 Spl/JHP	Winchester[3]	110	1044	10.0	.670	246
.357 Mag/JHP	Remington[4]	125	1450	12.25	.576	582

Notes:
1. Current (at time of testing) CHP ammunition
2. Current (at time of testing) FBI ammunition
3. Current (at time of testing) CHP ammunition
4. Current (at time of testing) CHP ammunition

California Highway Patrol Semiautomatic Pistol Report

In May 1990 the CHP Academy weapons training staff rendered its "Test and Evaluation: 10mm Semi-Automatic Pistol" report. It was immediately controversial for many reasons, but most noticeably because of its obvious predisposition.

Eight pistols from three manufacturers were tested:
1. Colt Model Double Eagle—10mm
2. Glock Model 20—10mm
3. Glock Model 22—.40 S&W
4. Glock Model 23—.40 S&W
5. Smith & Wesson Model 1006—10mm
6. Smith & Wesson Model 1076—10mm
7. Smith & Wesson Model 4006—.40 S&W
8. Smith & Wesson Model 4006 D/L—.40 S&W

Careful reading of the report reveals several instances wherein the testers' bias and predisposition were apparent. For this to be understood, however, one must remember that the CHP, like so many other law enforcement departments and agencies, has a long tradition of using nothing but Smith & Wesson sidearms. In the 1989 report, for example, a total of five weapons, of five different types, were tested, but all were manufactured by Smith & Wesson. In the CHP report, a total of twelve sample weapons were used, and eight (two-thirds) of them were manufactured by Smith & Wesson.

For some reason, CHP testers wanted their new pistols to be fairly traditional. The innovative Glock design was clearly too much for them. They rejected the double-action-only concept, and even the superior SIG-Sauer-type frame-mounted, decocking lever configuration. Evidently, they were willing to accept semiautomatics (not an entirely new concept for the CHP) but had trouble with much newness beyond that. They even had trouble with the brand-new .40 S&W cartridge, insisting on referring to it incorrectly as the "10mm Short." And, of course, they ended up recommending the Smith & Wesson Model 4006 with the "old style" slide-mounted combination safety/decocking lever.

Smith & Wesson 4006 chosen by the CHP.

Top: Smith & Wesson conventional Model 4006 selected by the CHP. Note the standard hammer and "flip-flap" slide-mounted safety/decocking lever. Center: Selective-double-action version. Note the bobbed hammer and SIG-Sauer-type decocking lever (black handle just forward of the grip panel and just below the slide stop lever). Bottom: Double-action-only version. Note the absence of a visible hammer and any slide- or frame-mounted safety or decocking levers.

Most professional firearms trainers, especially those who deal with tactical issues, have witnessed occurrences in the training environment in which those slide-mounted combination levers caused something that in a real life tactical situation would have gotten the shooter killed or gravely injured. That's why the FBI demanded that Smith & Wesson remove the thing from the Model 1006 before they adopted it, thus leading to the creation of the Model 1076. (By the way, those combination levers are not exclusive to Smith & Wesson pistols. They're also found on several other popular pistols, including Beretta 92s, many Walther models, and so on.)

Following the report's issuance, the California Highway Patrol initially purchased seven thousand Smith & Wesson Model 4006 pistols in the "standard safety model" (report's wording). During a telephone conversation shortly after the acquisition, Steve Melvin, then president of Smith & Wesson, told me he could not understand why any law enforcement department or agency would choose the "old style" slide-mounted safety/decocking lever configuration when the same weapon was available in either the frame-mounted decocking lever or the double-action-only configuration.

Glock and the CHP

The California Highway Patrol tested three models of Glock pistols: the 10mm Model 20, and the Models 22 and 23 in .40 S&W. As acknowledged in the report, all guns submitted for testing were preproduction samples. It can be seen clearly in the report's language, reproduced below in its entirety, that the testers were predisposed against Glock pistols and/or failed to understand them and their design.

Glock Model 20, 10 Millimeter
The Glock #20 10mm was returned to the

Glock Models 20 and 23, two of the pistols tested by the CHP.

factory immediately after its arrival due to excessive clearance found between extractor and bolt face causing it to malfunction during the initial inspection test firing. It was returned with the problem corrected on March 15 and its testing was resumed. The Glock was the only weapon submitted for testing that had no hammer. All of the Glock's firing mechanisms other than the trigger are contained inside the weapon's slide and grip frame. During the evaluation of the weapon design characteristics, it was noted that the magazine, whether loaded or empty, had to be physically extracted from the grip frame, never dropping free. The magazine follower also bound frequently inside the magazine body, occasionally causing difficulty loading, in some instances even preventing the loading of the magazine to its capacity. Later in the testing, the follower also worked its way completely out through the top of the magazine past the feed lips.

The Glock #20 exhibited the strongest recoil of all 10mm pistols tested. This made it the most difficult of all weapons to control when firing multiple shot groups. When it was fired by trainees who were being observed by the test staff, the consensus of opinion was that the recoil was excessive and too heavy for officers of smaller stature and hand size.

During the endurance firing, some 205 malfunctions were experienced with the Glock #20. The magazines always had to be removed from the weapon by hand, failing to drop free on their own. The malfunction rate for the Glock #20 was calculated to be one in every 19 rounds. Firing was halted at approximately 3,800 rounds because of severe cracking and deterioration of the bolt face at the firing pin opening, which caused repeated malfunctions. Additionally, upon final inspection of the weapon, cracks were found in the plastic frame rails adjacent to the magazine well at the rear of the barrel locking lug.

Glock Model 22, 10 Millimeter Short
(.40 S&W)

Two Glock #22 weapons were involved in this testing. The first suffered a barrel rupture due to a defective bullet fired during endurance testing. Subsequently a second weapon was provided and subjected to the entire test battery.

As with the Glock #20, the magazine had to be manually removed from the grip frame of the weapon during each magazine change. The recoil generated by the Glock #22 when firing the test round was second only to the smaller framed Glock #23. This recoil was found to be difficult to control when multiple shot groups were fired. When small-handed shooters fired the weapon, they all indicated that the recoil caused difficulty in control. The endurance test was completed with 37 recorded malfunctions, which resulted in a malfunction rate of one in every 137 rounds fired.

The weapon was cleaned and allowed to cool on four occasions due to malfunctions occurring from debris buildup. Upon completion of the test, the weapon was inspected by the Academy gunsmiths. During this inspection, cracks were found in the plastic frame rails adjacent to the magazine well at the rear of the barrel block.

Glock Model 23, 10 Millimeter Short (.40 S&W)

The Glock #23 was the lightest and smallest of all pistols tested. It, like the other Glocks, would not allow the magazine to drop free when released. The magazine follower could also be twisted and bound inside the magazine. Recoil from the Glock #23 was substantially higher than any other 10mm Short (.40 S&W) weapon fired. This resulted in much difficulty maintaining control when multiple shot groups were fired. The endurance testing of the Glock was halted at 1,038 rounds due to the breakage of the trigger spring rendering it incapable of continuing. To this point in the test, the Glock #23 has a malfunction rate of one in 25, experiencing 41 total malfunctions. Just as was found on the other Glock test weapons, the plastic frame was cracked adjacent to the magazine well behind the barrel locking block on the Glock #23. This was discovered during a final inspection of the weapon.

The testers' observations about the three Glock pistols tested make it clear that they were most bothered by two things: 1) that the magazines would not drop free and 2) that some cracks were discovered in the frame rails adjacent to the locking block.

The fact that the magazines do not drop free from Glock pistols has been an issue since the pistols first came to the United States and were discovered by competition shooters. The perception that this is a problem stems from certain competition disciplines where it has long been the technique of choice to change magazines during "combat" shooting by placing one's "weak" hand on a fresh magazine, then actuating the magazine release and allowing the old magazine to drop free while bringing the fresh one up toward the magazine well. Obviously, if the magazine in the gun doesn't drop free when the release is actuated, this technique won't work.

Comments on specific competition techniques aside, suffice it to say that their influence on serious law enforcement and personal defense tactics has gotten out of hand. When certain types of popular competitive games were conceived of a couple of decades ago, it was thought that if they were designed to resemble real-life tactical situations, the players would benefit from practicing them in more than one way. (Not a bad idea, but unfortunately, it was one that soon was lost.) Today such games bear little resemblance to real-life tactics in law enforcement and personal defense situations. The problem is that many competitors fail to realize this fact and/or refuse to admit its truth.

It's difficult, if not impossible, to find something designed by Gaston Glock that didn't turn out exactly the way he intended it. Magazines are no exception. Glock intentionally designed his pistol so that the magazines would not drop free. That's the way it turned out, and he has no intention of changing it, thank you.

The Salzburg Police, early purchasers of Glock pistols, issue only one magazine per pistol. The Austrian army, Glock's first customer, issues only two magazines per pistol to its soldiers, something not particularly unusual in various military forces around the world. That's why the Model 17 was designed and boxed to include two magazines—no more, no less. And underlying that is the reason the pistol was designed so the magazines would not drop free when the release was actuated. It was feared that soldiers with very little training (also not unusual in many military forces) would lose or damage magazines by dropping them inadvertently at inopportune times.

As for cracks in the frame rails adjacent to the locking block on the preproduction Models 20, 22, and 23, a few comments are in order. It must be noted that the pistols Glock sent were hand-delivered (by Karl Walter, vice president and head of Glock in the United States, and Al Bell, now director of training for Glock but then still with the Washington, D.C., police) prototypes that were provided with the understanding that they would not be used in the tests. But CHP used them anyway and, of course, experienced some problems that would not have occurred on production models. One such problem was the cracking on the receiver's slide rails near the locking block. Had CHP honored Glock's request and refrained from including the prototypes in the testing, there would have been no issue made of these because the production pistols (all calibers except 9mm) have a third pin (on the receiver, through the locking block, just above the trigger pin) that eliminates this cracking.

The CHP report states that the Model 20 malfunctioned 205 times in 3,800 rounds fired, or a malfunction rate of 1 in 19. For the Model 22 it reported 37 malfunctions in 5,000 rounds fired, or a malfunction rate of 1 in 137; and for the Model 23, 41 malfunctions were reported for 1,038 rounds fired, or a malfunction rate of 1 in 25.

Glock Model 20, the prototype of which was tested by the CHP.

The arrow points to the third pin on the Model 20. Production Models 20, 21, 22, and 23 all have third pins. The lack of this pin on the prototype Model 20 tested by the CHP contributed to cracks in the receiver.

The large rectangular piece in the photo's center is the locking block. The slide rails where CHP discovered cracks in the prototype are located on either side of the locking block.

That many instances of Glock pistols failing to fire are shooter-induced is a fact known by all certified Glock armorers, Glock police transition instructors, and properly trained law enforcement and civilian Glock shooters. Rather than being viewed as a defect in the pistol, this should be seen as the easily resolved result of a lack of training in the proper handling of a well-designed, well-built weapon. Shooter-induced stoppages in Glock pistols are so easily avoided that a properly trained Glock shooter will likely never experience one. But if it does happen, proper Glock training will likely result in it being immediately cleared so shooting can resume (see Chapter 14, "Operational Advantages," for more about this).

The shooter-induced stoppages are discussed in detail in Chapter 14. But for now it's appropriate to say that, like many other things, the CHP report failed to provide any details about the so-called malfunctions. How many were caused by ammunition failures? We know of at least one combination ammunition and shooter-caused failure in one of the Model 22s, when someone fired a second round after a squib round had lodged a bullet in the barrel. Also, how many of the CHP's reported "malfunctions" were stovepipes, something any properly trained Glock shooter knows is frequently shooter-induced, especially when the shooter's experience is limited mostly to revolvers?

Two police stories about Glock stoppages bear mentioning here. The first is again from Ayoob's *Guns* magazine articles. A Renton, Washington, police officer involved in a shoot-out got one shot off, then his Glock refused to fire any more. It was discovered by the officer's instructor that the officer had a cut on his "weak" hand thumb. The instructor believes it happened because the officer, reverting to old revolver habits in the heat of the moment, utilized a thumb-crossover two-hand hold and that the "weak" hand thumb was struck by the slide, cutting it and inducing a failure to cycle. Had the officer been trained properly and adequately, even if he'd reverted to the incorrect hold, he would have remedied the stoppage and been able to resume firing.

The other story comes from the San Francisco Police Department (SFPD). Not long after the board of supervisors refused to authorize funds to upgrade the SFPD's weapons from traditional revolvers to modern pistols (it wasn't money; the shortsighted supervisors and many San Francisco citizens seemed to feel that it would be dangerous for their police officers to have high-capacity 9mm pistols), one officer acquired his own Glock for off-duty use. Just a few days after beginning to carry it, he became involved in a robbery attempt at a local market. Attempting to stop the felon, he fired one shot, but his Glock wouldn't fire more. After it was all over (everything came out all right), the officer angrily contacted the seller and others, complaining about the fact that he had a single-shot Glock, not at all what he'd bargained for. Upon inspection of the weapon, it was immediately determined that he, being a revolver shooter with no pistol experience and no appropriate training on the Glock, had purchased the wrong ammunition. His Glock was loaded with 9mm Kurz, or .380 ACP, ammunition. Most guns would not even have chambered a single round, let alone fired one as his Glock had.

One often has only to be shown at least the basics about good equipment to realize the benefits it affords. The Glock is known among trainers and Glock shooters to be one of the "friendliest" pistols there is. Glocks are not only very comfortable (because of the design geometry, interrelationship of the bore axis and grip, "soft" polymer receiver, and well-balanced firing cycle), they are easy to operate effectively—far more so than traditional police-style revolvers (provided, of course, that at least a little foundation is given up front).

A case in point: Not long ago a class of recruits came through the San Francisco Sheriff's Academy and, much to everyone's dismay, a significant percentage failed to qualify using department-issue revolvers. The assistant training officer (ATO), a Glock owner, decided on the spot to try a little experiment. Upon questioning, all the recruits who had just failed to qualify revealed that they had never fired anything but revolvers. The ATO gave them a short lecture about Glocks, then asked each recruit, one by one, to refire the qualification course using his personal Glock. They all qualified the first time.

Who Cares?

No reasonable person can much care whether the California Highway Patrol ended up with the Smith & Wesson 4006 "standard safety model" instead of the Colt Double Eagle or one of the Glocks. After all, they're all decent weapons that would have served the CHP well. What's disturbing, however, is why the CHP behaved the way they did.

The CHP knew that Glock had rushed to get weapons to them and that those delivered were prototypes not to be utilized for testing. The CHP knew the guns Glock sent were merely examples to show what could be provided. The CHP agreed not to include those pistols in the testing. Nevertheless, they did include the Glocks in the test program. What's worse, they failed to provide any of the test staff or group of cadets utilized as test subjects with any familiarization or foundational training with Glock pistols.

Placing modern high-tech pistols in the hands of revolver shooters or those with little shooting experience without providing even a modicum of familiarization or foundational training is unconscionable. Moreover, it smacks of hardheaded machismo, the image of which good cops work hard to dispel. It's the sort of mentality that still considers guns a man's province; people who think that way believe that "real men" are born knowing how to shoot a gun and can pick up any one and do a credible job with it. There are names for such people: egotistical, bone-headed, male-chauvinistic, and, all too often, the dear departed.

Scottsdale Police Department Glock Semiautomatic Pistol Final Report

On 20 September 1991, Sergeant James M. Dray, training division supervisor and author of the Scottsdale Police Department report, presented it to Chief Fred Collins. This was the culmination of extensive research and testing, and it contained the following recommendation: "After examining a variety of available weapons, both the training unit supervisor and the department rangemaster have selected the Glock pistol as the recommended semiautomatic pistol which should be issued as the only authorized duty weapon for the Scottsdale Police Department."

Before the Scottsdale testing was concluded on 26 July 1990, Sgt. Dray learned about the California Highway Patrol report, including the fact that the CHP had declared the Glock pistols to have failed their testing and had specifically identified the problems of controllability, slide rail cracking, excessive recoil, and magazine not falling free.

Concerned, he contacted the CHP hoping to get information that would be helpful with Scottsdale PD's selection process. He was put in touch with an Officer Jones (not one of the six CHP Academy weapons staff members who participated in the test, but that was unknown to Dray at that time). Jones told Dray some things that were contained in the CHP report but, when a copy was requested, claimed one was not available to Scottsdale PD. Also, Jones denied that Glock had ever advised the CHP not to test the submitted pistols.

Officer Jones of the CHP did not quit there. He told Dray that the Mesa Police Department had tested the .40-caliber Glock and experienced the same problems as the CHP. Dray contacted Mesa PD and was told that was untrue, that the Mesa PD did not test the .40-caliber Glock.

Four days later Sgt. Dray contacted Glock in Smyrna, Georgia, and was told, among other things, that modifications had been made as a result of the CHP testing. It was also suggested that Dray contact the South Carolina Law Enforcement Division (SLED), because they'd had .40-caliber Glocks since May 1990 and had experienced no problems at all.

The next day Dray contacted a Captain Henderson at SLED and was told that they had "not experienced any of the problems cited in the CHP report," although Henderson was not then aware of the report. Dray reports that Henderson "advised that the pistol has been well received by all members of the department and they have not experienced any real training problems."

Scottsdale PD decided to subject the .40-caliber Glock

pistol to the same 5,000-round firing test that the CHP had. The following is from the Scottsdale report:

On July 31, 1990, Officer Furr advised that he had fired 500 rounds of ammunition in the pistol (a Glock Model 22) without cleaning or allowing it to cool down. Furr advised that there were no malfunctions or cracking of the slide rails. Officer Furr advised that he is confident that the problem has been corrected. He further advised that he would make arrangements for us to obtain a facility to do the 5,000 round testing when the ammunition arrives.

On August 2, 1990, Mr. Jeff Langhorst, area representative for Glock, called to advise that Glock has shipped a .40-caliber pistol and 500 rounds of ammunition. Additionally, he advised that he was present with Officer Furr for additional testing of the Glock at the Phoenix Range. On August 1, 1990, Langhorst advised that a total of 1,000 rounds have been fired through the pistol without a malfunction. This was in spite of the fact that the pistol had not been cleaned.

On August 8, 1990, myself, Officers Haenel and Cervantes met Officer Furr at the Mesa Police Department Range for the purpose of completing the mandated testing (5,000 rounds). Furr advised that he had completed firing 1,750 rounds without any malfunctions.

At 0815 hours we began our testing. At the completion of each 500 rounds the pistol was taken apart and completely cleaned. This procedure was followed throughout the testing. At 1315 hours the testing was completed with a total of 5,000 rounds of ammunition having been fired (3,250 on this date).

The following observations were made at the conclusion of this inspection:

No cracks were found to the slide rails or any other areas of the frame (plastic).

The firing pin spacer sleeve was found to have begun to develop a crack. This would not cause the pistol to fail and this part would be scheduled for routine replacement at 2,000 rounds.

The slide was observed to have developed some wear due to the locking block striking it during normal operation. Mr. Garrett advised that there was some metal fatigue involved which was minor and did not appear to present a potential problem.

Furr advised that Glock has been aware of this wear and has advised that this is not a problem. This will not interfere with the operation of the slide.

As a result of this mandated testing and inspection the following observations are made:

Of the 5,000 rounds, three were found to be defective and replaced.

Three operator induced malfunctions were experienced during the testing. On these occasions the officer allowed his thumb to ride up the frame and trip the slide stop lever, which engaged the slide and locked it in the rear position, which is what the lever is supposed to do. This is a training issue and will be addressed at that time. It should be noted that this only occurred after the officer had fired several magazines and was feeling fatigued.

No feeding, extracting, or ejecting malfunctions were experienced throughout the testing.

The inspection revealed what would be considered less than normal wear to the pistol.

> Based on the firing test and the lab inspection it is the decision of the training staff that the concerns listed in the CHP report have been corrected, as Glock had advised, and the pistol far exceeds the expectations and is acceptable as the department issued duty weapon.

The California Highway Patrol was, at the time of this writing, transitioning to its new Smith & Wesson Model 4006s; two years was the estimated time it would take to phase in seven thousand new weapons statewide.

CHP is very pleased with its choice and stands by its report and the evaluation of Glock pistols contained therein.

Scottsdale PD officially adopted the Glock Models 22 and 23 as of 1 January 1991, and it, too, is pleased with its decision and stands by its report.

The merits of CHP's report and/or the ethics of its testing aside, it seems that one need not trash something that is very popular among one's peers simply to justify one's desire to select something else instead. Certainly no other law enforcement agency or police department that decided against Glock pistols resorted to such unprofessional "Glock bashing."

On the other hand, the Scottsdale report was not included here because it was the only favorable report extant. Quite the contrary, there is an abundance of commendatory reports. The Scottsdale report was included specifically because it refers directly to—and was written in response to—the CHP report.

Who is right and who is wrong? That is something each of us must decide for ourselves. For more information upon which to base such a decision, see Chapter 5, "Can 3,500 Departments Be Wrong?"

Can 3,500 Departments Be Wrong?

s mentioned in previous chapters, as of spring 1991, 3,500 federal, state, and local law enforcement departments and agencies in the United States had adopted or approved Glock pistols for duty use. At the end of this chapter is a partial list—covering only the acquisition period between June 1986 and July 1989—of those departments and agencies.

The New York State Police

The January-February 1990 issue of *The Trooper*, the official publication of the New York State Police (NYSP), ran an article entitled "Glock 17 Becomes New Division-Issue Sidearm." The article begins by stating what many already know, that a terrible drug problem "has permeated our society in the past decade, and with it a wave of violence and ruthlessness that we never could have predicted. This epidemic and violence have touched every facet of our lives."

The article goes on to say: ". . . a trooper armed with a six-shot revolver . . . is grossly disadvantaged in terms of firepower, and in terms of being able to quickly reload." Also reported is an example—two troopers who responded to a request to back up a federal officer. When they arrived on scene, "an assailant . . . posing as the federal officer, suddenly pulled a semi-automatic pistol and began firing as they were talking. The assailant fired numerous shots but neither trooper was able to return fire, due in part to the sustained firing capability of the assailant's semi-automatic pistol."

New York State Police logo.

The article then references the superintendent's earlier (1989) message that an intensive research program was underway to evaluate the adequacy of the division's issue sidearm (a .357 Magnum revolver). The superintendent mandated that any new issue sidearm "be easy and safe to use and provide the greatest capability for self-protection."

Can 3,500 Departments Be Wrong?

The official publication of the NYSP.

The New York State Police testing and evaluation program was conducted from June 1988 through September 1989. At first, eleven weapons were selected for evaluation, but two were considered too complicated, requiring excessive training time, and were thus dropped from the program. That left the Beretta 92F, the Beretta 92F Compact, the Glock 17, Smith & Wesson Models 659, 669, and 459, the Ruger P-85, and SIG-Sauer Models P226 and P225.

Evaluations were conducted by a variety of division members (three of whom were female), including five troopers, one sergeant, two Bureau of Criminal Investigation field members, and five recruit troopers then in the academy. "Division firearms instructors were not included among the evaluators to assure that the test results would be based on the opinions of members having neither specific knowledge of, nor preference for, a particular weapon or manufacturer." It's too bad the California Highway Patrol lacked such wisdom. Testing was accomplished using all weapons "out of the box" with no lubrication or maintenance before or during any phase. "This was done to help identify the quality of workmanship and sensitivity to malfunction . . ." Sixteen feature categories were established to rate each weapon: finish, slide action, trigger pull, safety, weight and balance empty, grip size, magazine release mechanism, magazine loading, slide release mechanism, disassembly/reassembly, weight and balance loaded, grip finish, sights, recoil, magazine removal/insertion, and muzzle flash. More than 1,800 rounds were fired through each test weapon during the evaluation process.

At that point in the testing and evaluation process, division members identified something "deemed to be an extremely important feature for any Division-issue semi-automatic sidearm, that being a double-action-only trigger mechanism. This feature allows consistent trigger pulls and requires no decocking of the hammer after firing in order to reholster the weapon in a safe condition."

It was determined that only one of the test weapons actually met the criteria. As a result, manufacturers of the other weapons were contacted to see if they would or could supply pistols that complied. Some declined and "refused any attempt to modify their weapons." Other manufacturers agreed to try to produce a double-action-only pistol. Eventually, three manufacturers were able to produce a double-action-only pistol, so NYSP had a total of four weapons with which to complete the testing and evaluation process.

Using those four, the division prepared specifications for an issue pistol and put out bids in October 1989. The following month, it awarded Glock the contract for the Model 17, which would become the only New York State Police duty sidearm for all 3,900 uniform and undercover personnel. Soon thereafter deliveries began and Glock

17s started getting into the hands of New York State Police troopers. By March 1990, the last of the 4,300 Model 17 pistols contracted for had been delivered.

South Carolina Law Enforcement Division

The South Carolina Law Enforcement Division was formed in 1947 to provide sophisticated services (such as forensics and special investigation) to local police departments and other law enforcement agencies throughout the state. These days SLED is also in the business of dealing with narcotics and dangerous drugs, and there is a Criminal Justice Information and Communications System as well. The head honcho, presently Chief Robert Stewart, reports directly to the governor of South Carolina, presently Carroll P. Campbell, Jr.

Through the end of 1989 SLED agents were permitted to carry (on duty or off) whatever sidearm they chose, so long as they could qualify with it. Not surprisingly, the most common weapons of choice for most of SLED's history were traditional .38 Special and .357 Magnum revolvers. But in recent years that started to change until, by the end of the 1980s, wheelguns were carried by less than one-third of the three hundred agents. Also not surprisingly, semiautos were growing rapidly in popularity, especially .45s (Colt Government Models and SIG-Sauer P220s) and the 9mm Glock 17.

As many agencies and departments have discovered, such a myriad of weaponry poses a tactical nightmare. So, in keeping with the trend, SLED decided to standardize its agents' sidearms by making a single make and model pistol mandatory.

SLED's original selection criteria list required that the new gun be: 1) a double-action-only pistol; 2) suitable for all physical, tactical, and meteorological conditions agents would likely encounter; 3) caliber 9mm Parabellum (optional larger caliber available); 4) minimum

12-round magazine capacity; 5) no magazine disconnect; 6) maximum loaded weight 2.5 pounds; 7) wear- and rust-resistant finish; 8) optional night sights available; and 9) optional compact version available.

Five pistols made it to the final phase:
1. SIG-Sauer P220
2. Smith & Wesson Model 5906
3. Smith & Wesson Model 6906
4. Glock Model 17
5. Glock Model 19

It was planned that two pistols would be adopted, essentially a standard size and a compact version of the same gun. In canvassing agents about their choice of frame size and other things, it became apparent that more than half were unsatisfied with the 9mm Parabellum criterion; they wanted a larger caliber.

SLED Lieutenant James B. McClary, head of weapons training, had visited the FBI Academy during the time the Firearms Training Unit was conducting tests that eventually resulted in their selection of the 10mm (FBI Lite) cartridge. At some point thereafter, McClary suggested that SLED change its caliber criterion so that 10mm would be the caliber of choice. It almost happened, but at that time all pistols large enough to accommodate the 10mm round exceeded SLED's size and weight criteria.

So SLED chose the Glock Models 17 and 19 because they'd outperformed the others in all respects. Reputedly, the evaluating agents qualified as well or better with the relatively unfamiliar Glocks as they had with their comfortable old wheelguns.

They almost got their 9mm Glocks but, before they did, Glock announced the introduction of the Models 22 and 23 in .40 caliber. SLED firearms trainers went to the Smyrna, Georgia, factory in January 1990 to attend the Glock Armorer's and Police Transition Instructor courses and, while there, learned that Glock could deliver .40-

caliber guns in May. McClary and the other agents returned home and proposed that SLED change its order with Glock from the 9mm pistols to the .40-caliber ones. And so it did.

SLED agents were permitted to choose either the Model 22 or the Model 23 as their duty sidearm. The larger model was chosen by 82 percent, while only 18 percent went for the smaller Model 23.

One of the 40-caliber Glock pistols that went to SLED.

As promised, SLED began receiving the first production pistols in early May 1990 and, as such, became the world's first law enforcement agency to adopt a .40-caliber Glock and the new .40 S&W ammunition. By August 1990 SLED had completed transition training for all its agents, thereby achieving yet another first: it was the first agency to put a .40-caliber pistol into law enforcement service.

PARTIAL U.S.A. AGENCY GLOCK PISTOLS
CONFIDENTIAL REFERENCE LISTING
* * * * * * * * * *

(Acquisition Period June 1986-July 1989)

STATE	AGENCY	MODEL	COMMENTS
CA	Arcadia Police Dept.	G17	Duty Weapon

TX	Arlington Police Dept.	G17, G19	Proposed 1989
VA	Arlington Police Dept.	G17, G19	Under Evaluation
MA	Auburn Police Dept.	G17	Duty Weapon
NJ	Atlantic City Police Dept.	G19	Duty Weapon
TX	Austin Police Dept.	G17, G19	Duty Weapon
NJ	Barrington Police Dept.	G17	Duty Weapon
KY	Berea Police Dept.	G17	Duty Weapon
IA	Bettendorf Police Dept.	G17	Duty Weapon
MI	Birmingham Police Dept.	G17, G19	Admin. Duty Weapon
MA	Boston Police Dept.	G17, G19	Proposed 1989/90
MA	Boxboro Police Dept.	G17	Duty Weapon
CT	Bristol Police Dept.	G17	Duty Weapon
MA	Brockton Police Dept.	G17	Duty Weapon
MA	Burlington Police Dept.	G17	Duty Weapon
TX	Carrollton Police Dept.	G17	Duty Weapon
GA	Chamblee Police Dept.	G17	Duty Weapon
NC	Chapel Hill Police Dept.	G17	Duty Weapon
MA	Chelmsford Police Dept.	G17	Duty Weapon
GA	Cobb County Park Rangers	G17	Duty Weapon
GA	College Park Police Dept.	G17	Duty Weapon
MA	Commonwealth of Massachusetts Metropolitan Police	G17, G19	Duty Weapon
FL	Coral Gables Police Dept.	G17, G19	Duty Weapon
TX	Dallas County Sheriff's Dept.	G17, G19	Duty Weapon
TX	Dallas Police Dept.	G17, G19	Authorized Duty Weapon
MA	Danvers Police Dept.	G17	Duty Weapon
OH	Dayton Police Dept.	G17	Duty Weapon
NH	Dover Police Dept.	G17	Duty Weapon
IN	Elkhart Police Dept.	G17	Duty Weapon
NJ	Englewood Cliffs Police Dept.	G17	Duty Weapon
WA	Everett Police Dept.	G17	Duty Weapon
NH	Farmington Police Dept.	G17	Duty Weapon
FL	Flagler Co. Sheriff's Dept.	G17	Duty Weapon
AZ	Flagstaff Police Department	G17	Duty Weapon
CO	Ft. Collins Police Dept.	G17	Duty Weapon
CT	Glastonbury Police Dept.	G19	Duty Weapon
IN	Goshen Police Dept.	G17	Duty Weapon
NJ	Hackensack Police Dept.	G17, G19	Duty Weapon
CT	Hamden Police Dept.	G17	Duty Weapon
NH	Hampton Police Dept.	G17	Duty Weapon
MA	Harwich Police Dept.	G17	Duty Weapon
FL	Havana Police Dept.	G17	Duty Weapon
FL	Hialeah Police Dept.	G17, G19	Duty Weapon
MD	Howard Co. Police Dept.	G17	Authorized Duty Weapon
MI	Kalamazoo Police Dept.	G17	Authorized Duty Weapon
KS	Kansas City Police Dept.	G17	Tactical Unit
NH	Keene Police Dept.	G17	Duty Weapon
WA	King County Police Dept.	G17	Authorized Duty Weapon

Can 3,500 Departments Be Wrong?

IN	LaGrange Police Dept.	G17	Duty Weapon
CA	La Mesa Police Dept.	G17	Duty Weapon
MI	Lansing Police Dept.	G17, G19	Duty Weapon
FL	Long Boat Key Police Dept.	G17	Duty Weapon
MA	Lynn Police Dept.	G17, G19	Duty Weapon
GA	Madison Police Dept.	G17	Duty Weapon
NH	Manchester Police Dept.	G17	Duty Weapon
GA	Marietta Police Dept.	G17	Duty Weapon
NJ	Maywood Police Dept.	G19	Duty Weapon
TX	McAllen Police Dept.	G17	Duty Weapon
MA	Mendon Police Dept.	G17	Duty Weapon
FL	Metro Dade Police Dept.	G17, G19	Best Test Results
FL	Miami Police Dept.	G17, G19	Duty Weapon
MI	Mt. Clemens Police Dept.	G17	Duty Weapon
MA	New Bedford Police Dept.	G17	Duty Weapon
NY	New York City Police Dept.	G19	Police Administrators, OCCB
AZ	Nogales Police Dept.	G17, G19	Duty Weapon
MA	Northhampton Police Dept.	G19	Duty Weapon
OH	Oakwood Police Dept.	G17	Tactical Unit
UT	Odgen Police Dept.	G17	Duty Weapon
MI	Ottawa Co. Sheriff's Dept.	G17, G19	Duty Weapon
NJ	Paramus Police Dept.	G17, G19	Duty Weapon
PA	Philadelphia Police Dept.	G17, G10	Authorized Duty Weapon
AZ	Phoenix Police Dept.	G17, G19	Duty Weapon
SD	Pierre Police Dept.	G17, G19	Duty Weapon
PA	Pittsburgh Police Dept.	G17, G19	Under Evaluation
MN	Ramsey Sheriff's Dept.	G17, G19	Duty Weapon
NJ	Roselle Police Dept.	G17	Duty Weapon
CA	Sacramento Sheriff's Dept.	G17, G19	Authorized Duty Weapon
CA	San Diego Co. Marshal	G17, G19	Authorized Duty Weapon
CA	San Francisco Police Dept.	G17, G19	Authorized Duty Weapon
UT	San Juan Sheriff's Dept.	G17	Duty Weapon
CA	Santa Cruz Sheriff's Dept.	G17	Duty Weapon
FL	Sarasota Police Dept.	G17	Duty Weapon
WA	Seattle Police Dept.	G17, G19	Authorized Duty Weapon
LA	Shreveport Police Dept.	G17	Duty Weapon
GA	Smyrna Police Dept.	G17, G19	Duty Weapon
CA	Sonoma Co. Sheriff's Dept.	G17	Authorized Duty Weapon
WA	Spokane Police Dept.	G17, G19	Summer1989
OR	Springfield Police Dept.	G17	Duty Weapon
MN	St. Paul Police Dept.	G17, G19	Duty Weapon
FL	St. Petersburg Police Dept.	G17, G19	Duty Weapon
FL	State of Fla. Dept. of Natural Resources (Marine Patrol)	G17	Duty Weapon
GA	State of Georgia Kennesaw College Police	G17	Duty Weapon
KS	State of Kansas ABC Unit	G17, G19	Duty Weapon

MD	State of Maryland	G17	Best Test Results
MN	State of Minnesota	G17, G19	Best Test Results
NJ	State of New Jersey	G17, G19	
	Dept. of Environmental Protection	G17	Duty Weapon
	Dept. of Corrections	G17	Under Evaluation
NY	State of New York	G17	Under Evaluation
TN	State of Tennessee		
	Bureau of Investigations	G19	Duty Weapon
	Office of Attorney General	G19	Duty Weapon
UT	State of Utah		
	University Police	G17	Duty Weapon
VT	State of Vermont	G17	Best Test Results
MI	Sterling Hts. Police Dept.	G17, G19	Duty Weapon
NY	Suffern Police Dept.	G17	Duty Weapon
WA	Tacoma Police Dept.	G17	Duty Weapon
FL	Tampa Police Dept.	G17	Duty Weapon
MA	Tewksbury Police Dept.	G19	Duty Weapon
WY	Torrington Police Dept.	G17	Duty Weapon
CT	Town of Hamden Police Dept.	G17, G19	Duty Weapon
MI	Troy Police Dept.	G17, G19	Duty Weapon
GA	Union City Police Dept.	G17	Duty Weapon
MN	Univ. of Minn. Police Dept.	G17	Duty Weapon
MA	Wakefield Police Dept.	G17	Duty Weapon
IA	Washington Co. Sheriff's Dept.	G17	Duty Weapon
DC	Washington Metro Police Dept.	G17, G19	Duty Weapon
MI	Washtenaw Co. Sheriff's Dept.	G17	Tactical Unit
CT	Waterford Police Dept.	G17	Duty Weapon
MA	Wayland Police Dept.	G17	Duty Weapon
ME	Wells Police Dept.	G17	Duty Weapon
UT	West Valley Police Dept.	G17, G19	Duty Weapon
MA	Weymouth Police Dept.	G17	Duty Weapon
CT	Windsor Police Dept.	G17	Duty Weapon
MA	Woburn Police Dept.	G17, G19	Duty Weapon

U.S. Government Agencies

MI	Dept. of Defense (Detroit)		
	Criminal Investigation Svc.	G19	Authorized Duty Weapon
DC	U.S. Dept. of Justice		
	Border Patrol	G17, G19	Authorized Duty Weapon
	DEA	G17, G19	Authorized Duty Weapon
	Immigr. & Nat. Svc.	G17, G19	Authorized Duty Weapon
	Marshal Services	G17	Authorized Duty Weapon
	U.S. Distr. Atty. Office, Miami	G17, G19	Duty Weapon
	Dept. of the Navy		
	Criminal Invest. Svc.	G17, G19	Under Evaluation
DC	U.S. Dept of State (Outside U.S.)		
	Diplomatic Security	G17, G19	Authorized Duty Weapon

Can 3,500 Departments Be Wrong?

DC	U.S. Dept.. of Treasury		
	U.S. Customs Service	G17, G19	Authorized Duty Weapon /Under Evaluation
	U.S. IRS	G17, G19	Authorized Duty Weapon
	U.S. INS	G17, G19	Authorized Duty Weapon
	FLETC	G17	Issue Weapon
	U.S. Dept. of Interior		
	Park Police	G17	Under Evaluation
	U.S. Postal Service	G17, G19	Duty Weapon
	Naval Investigative Service	G17, G19	Authorized Duty Weapon

International Agencies

Austria	Armed Forces	G17	Standard Sidearm
	Federal Police	G17	Standard Sidearm
	Special Police	G17	Standard Sidearm
Belgium	Schaerbeek Police	G17	Standard Sidearm
Canada	Armed Forces	G19	Under Evaluation
	QPP Sûreté du Quebec		
	Montreal		Tactical Units
	Toronto PD	G17, G19	Special Units
	Waterloo PD, Ontario	G17	Tactical Units
Ecuador	Security Staff	G17	Standard Sidearm
Great Britain	London Metro. Police Dept.	G17	First Unit Delivery
	London Police Dept.	G17	First Unit Delivery
Hong Kong	Royal Hong Kong Police	G17	Standard Sidearm
India	Special Protection Grp.	G17	Standard Sidearm
	National Security Guard	G17	Standard Sidearm
Italy	Air Force Security	G17	Duty Weapon
Jordan	Presidential Guard	G17	Standard Sidearm
Netherlands	(NATO)	G17	First Army Order Delivered
Norway	Armed Forces (NATO)	G17	Standard Sidearm
			NATO Stk. #100t-25-133-6775
Philippines	Presidential Guard	G17	Standard Sidearm
	PAFSECOM	G17	Standard Sidearm
	NICA	G17	Standard Sidearm
	NBI	G17	Standard Sidearm
Taiwan	Garrison Command	G17	Standard Sidearm
Thailand	CIB (Police)	G17	Standard Sidearm
Venezuela	Commandos CAVIM	G17	Standard Sidearm
West Germany	GSG 9	G17	Best Results in 2 yrs. of International Tests
Mexico	Secretaria de la Marina	G17	Standard Sidearm

After this list was made the count was, at the time of this writing in May 1991, 3,500 departments and agencies and 200,000 cops with Glocks. Who knows to what extent those numbers will have grown by the time you read this? Can these thousands of departments and agencies, and hundreds of thousands of cops, be wrong?

CHAPTER 6

9mm Glock Pistols: The Ones That Started It All

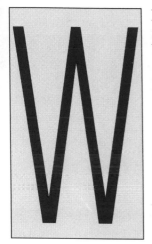

hen Gaston Glock produced his very first pistol in 1982, it was chambered in 9mm Parabellum (also called 9 x 19, 9mm Luger, and 9mm NATO). That was the Model 17.

Despite the fact that Gaston Glock and his original band of advisors likely never conceived of an entire line of pistols flowing from the Model 17, it has come to pass. Not only are there currently three more in 9mm Parabellum caliber, there are four more in three other calibers.

All in all, Glock produces eight models, numbered 17 through 23. Half of them utilize the original Model 17's receiver essentially unchanged. Of those four—Models 17, 17L, 18, and 22—all but the Model 22 are chambered for the 9mm Parabellum round.

Model 17

The Model 17 weighs 21.91 ounces empty, with no magazine installed. That's remarkably little for a high-capacity (17-round magazine, as originally designed) semiautomatic handgun. The empty magazine adds only 2.08 ounces, and the whole kit and caboodle—pistol, magazine, and 18 rounds of 9mm JHP defense-type ammunition—tips the scales at a mere 31.41 ounces. That's only 1.51 ounces more than an empty SIG-Sauer P226, and 2.59 ounces less than an empty Beretta 92F.

The Model 17 Glock is 7.21 inches long, measured at the slide, its longest part. The barrel is 4.49 inches long. Including the rear sight, the pistol is 5.16 inches high without a magazine installed.

Glock Model 17 with standard-capacity magazine and adjustable sights.

The standard magazine adds only about .031 inch to the pistol's overall height, but the "+2" magazine not only makes the gun taller, it changes the height profile altogether. A "+2" magazine (in reality just a different floorplate in place of the original) adds about .094 inch of height at the rear of the magazine, but a whopping .375 inch at the front.

Glock's first pistol is only 1.18 inches wide—nice and flat, even among semiautomatic handguns known for their trimness in that regard. While detractors are quick to point out the relatively broad girth of pistols designed to accommodate double-column (staggered) magazines, they fail to note that among these, Glocks are devoid of external switches and levers—gadgets that increase both the width of a pistol and its propensity to snag clothing and other things to which it comes in close proximity.

Shooting comfort is something Glock pistols are known for, and the Model 17 may be the most comfortable of them all. Certainly it is the most popular, if numbers sold mean anything.

Model 17L

Not many people have had the pleasure of shooting a long-slide Glock pistol, but those who have really like them. The Model 17L is Glock's original attempt at a competition version of the old standby Model 17.

The receiver is identical in all respects. In fact, you could own a Model 17

Glock's long-slide Model 17L.

and a Model 17L slide and convert back and forth merely by swapping slides on the same receiver. Some people actually do that, using the standard configuration as a "working gun" for home or workplace defense most of the time, then converting to long slide configuration on weekends for a little competitive shooting.

Even though the Model 17 and 17L receivers themselves are identical, there are two different items on a factory Model 17L: 1) an extended magazine catch, and 2) a 3 1/2-pound connector. A person wishing to utilize a single receiver with two slides in the manner described above could also switch the magazine catches and connectors each time the slides were swapped. Even though the actual switching is simple and both can be done in two or three minutes, there is a complication.

Glock's policy is to provide 3 1/2-pound connectors only on Model 17Ls. They generally will not sell a connector by itself, even to certified Glock armorers; they want the receiver shipped to them so they can install it (some earlier Model 17Ls were sold with 5-pound connectors). This is not a legal consideration; it is Glock company policy only. If a person were to install a 3 1/2-pound connector in a standard Model 17—or any other model, for that matter—no law would be broken. Glock, however, is very liability conscious and believes that a pistol with such a light trigger pull is inappropriate for anything except competition.

This same policy consideration does not apply to extended magazine catches. Glock has no liability concerns about which pistols these are installed on, despite the fact that some people believe an extended magazine catch is unwise for a defense pistol because it can more easily snag on clothing and more readily facilitate unintentional release. The other side of this argument, however, is that since Glock pistols do not have magazine safeties and their magazines are designed not to drop freely when released, an unintentional release, even if it were to occur, would not be catastrophic.

Model 17L slides are 8.77 inches long, 1.56 inches longer than the slide on a standard Model 17. The barrel itself is 6.02 inches, 1.53 inches longer than standard. The long slide features a rectangular opening on top. It begins immediately behind the front sight, is just a hair more than 2 1/2 inches long, and is as wide as the top of the slide. This opening reduces overall weight, especially near the muzzle, and it helps cool the barrel during extended firing such as often occurs in competition.

Many competitors prefer to increase the muzzle weight of their pistols, supposedly to facilitate sight reacquisition during multiple-shot firing sequences. There is an entire aftermarket industry supplying drop-in, add-on, and customized modifications for competition pistols. Some competitors spend as much as $5,000 to $10,000 modifying their pistols. But none of these high-priced custom jobs are done on Glock pistols. (The little that is available to modify Glocks for competition is covered in Chapter 15.)

The 6.02-inch-long barrel currently shipped on Model 17Ls is identical to the standard 4.49-inch Model 17 barrel except for the 1.53 additional inches. Earlier Model 17Ls were shipped with ported barrels, but these have been discontinued. The ports were three lateral slots cut in the top half of the barrel, supposedly to provide some compensation for muzzle rise. (Directing some of the combustion gasses upward causes a corresponding downward force vector to oppose the pistol's natural tendency to go muzzle-up during firing.)

In early 1990, Glock stopped producing ported barrels for the Model 17L and began shipping only solid, non-ported barrels. There has been considerable speculation about why Glock abandoned the ported barrels, usually with some suggestion that barrels were cracking. Factory personnel insist that the decision to stop producing ported barrels had little to do with cracking problems. Evidently, there were a few cases of small cracks. These reportedly occurred in the sharp corners where the porting cuts were made in the barrels. Relieving the sharp corners with radii presumably would have cured the problem, but for reasons of their own (probably economic), Glock decided to produce only nonported barrels. (For more on ported barrel problems, see Chapter 7, "Model 18: The Invisible Glock.")

Model 19

In 1988 Glock began producing the Model 19. A so-called compact version of the Model 17, the Model 19 is virtually identical except that it's about half an inch (.47 inch) shorter in length, and about a quarter inch (.24 inch) shorter in height.

Right-side view of the Glock Model 19, equipped with standard-capacity magazine and adjustable sights.

The same Model 19, viewed from the left side.

The Model 19 weighs about 4 percent (.92 ounce) less than the Model 17 when both are empty and without magazines. Because the Model 19 has only a 4.02-inch barrel, .47 inch shorter than the Model 17's, its sight radius is also shorter: 5.98 inches compared to the Model 17's 6.50 inches.

The Model 19 comes with 15-round magazines compared to its big brother's 17-rounders. With +2 floor-plates, magazine capacities obviously increase to 17 and 19 rounds respectively. Thus, a Model 19 equipped with a +2 magazine holds the same quantity of ammunition as the original-configuration Model 17. More importantly, Model 19s accept the larger Model 17 magazines and function normally with them. The significance of this is that where compactness is an issue, as in concealed-carry situations, the 15- or 17-round Model 19 magazines serve well. On the other hand, where concealment is not an issue, such as for home or workplace defense, the tactically superior 19-round Model 17 +2 magazine does a

fine job. Such combi-
nations are common
among users of Glock
pistols.

An Unusual Model 19

As stated before, the original
Glock pistol, the Model 19, was chambered for standard 9mm Parabellum (also
known as 9 x 19) ammunition. Since then,
all 9mm Glocks have left the factory chambered for the same
size ammunition.

In recent times a
few competitors
have modified the
chambers of their 9mm
Glocks to accommodate the
slightly longer 9 x 21 cartridge. Doing
this allows the pistol to accept ammunition that can be loaded a bit more powerfully in an attempt to "make major" (qualify to compete in the category for the most
powerful
guns), as
some com-
petitors say.
Such modi-
fications, needless to say, are
done without factory sanction.

But the Glock factory did
actually produce three Model 19s
chambered for the European 9 x 21 cartridge.

Three Special Agents of the U.S.

Glock Models 19, 17, and 17L (top to bottom).

88

Naval Investigative Service who happened to be stationed in Italy were about to acquire Glocks for their sidearms. It occurred to them that the nature of their work—incognito much of the time, often without military identification—was such that problems would eventually ensue if they carried 9mm NATO-chambered weapons, which are illegal for civilians in Italy. Bizarre as it may seem, however, the 9 x 21 cartridge is not illegal for civilians, so the three guys from NIS, stationed in Naples, contacted Alfonso Giambelli, the Glock representative located in Milano. Eventually the word came down that it could be done, and soon they had their pistols.

Special Agent Guy Molina's unusual Model 19, chambered for 9 x 21 ammunition.

A closer look at the unusual slide markings of Molina's Model 19.

A standard 9 x 19 chamber (left) and Molina's 9 x 21 chamber (right). Molina's pistol uses very crude GECO 9 x 21 ammunition.

A Winchester 9 x 19 JHP (left) compared to the GECO 9 x 21 cartridge (right).

The first of the three went to Special Agent Guy A. Molina. It bears the Italian catalog number 5693, but it also has a U.S. serial number—EN262US. The other two special pistols are numbered EN261US and EN262US. These are the only three such Glocks in existence.

They'll only function reliably with FMJ bullets in 9 x 21, but they will handle all 9 x 19 ammunition the same as any other Model 19. When the accompanying photographs were taken, some extractor erosion was noted. It is unknown at this time whether or not this was due to firing 9 x 21 ammunition, but a new extractor was installed when we took the photos, and time will tell.

Frontal view of a 9mm standard-capacity magazine (left) and a 9mm +2 magazine (right).

9mm Magazines

Glock produces three 9mm magazine bodies: 15-, 17-, and 31-round capacities. Installing a +2 floorplate increases the total capacity of each of these.

The large magazine currently comes equipped only with the +2 floorplate, giving it a 33-round capacity. Although it functions quite well in Models 17, 17L, and 19, it was originally intended for use in the Model 18. The 33-round magazine is sold only to law enforcement departments, per Glock policy.

Rear view of the 9mm +2 magazine (right) and the 9mm standard-capacity magazine (left). Note that both have only 17-round indicators. This is because only the floorplate is different on a +2 magazine; the body containing round indicators is the same.

9mm Barrels

All 9mm Glock barrels have Glock's exclusive hexagonal rifling with right-hand twist that is almost 1-in-10. Actually, Glock's 9mm rifling causes a bullet to make one 360-degree rotation in every 9.84 inches of travel.

• • • • •

Standard-capacity floorplate (left) and +2 floorplate (right).

With the advent of larger-caliber Glock pistols, some doomsayers have predicted the demise of 9mm Glocks. But merely producing guns in additional calibers (a practice long followed by other manufacturers) is highly unlikely to cause the market for Glock's 9mm pistols to dry up, since 9mm Parabellum ammunition is so widely used around the world. On the contrary, all indications are that the Glocks that started it all—the Models 17 and 19—will be around for a long time to come.

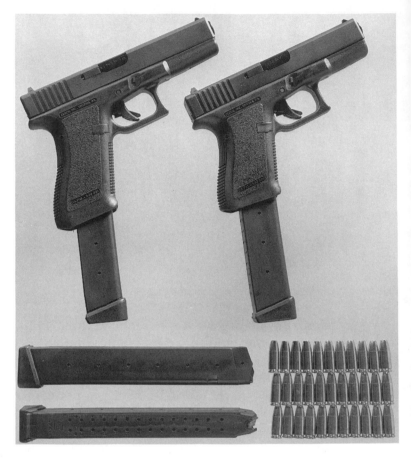

Glock Models 17 and 19 shown with Glock 33-round magazines.

CHAPTER 7

Model 18: The Invisible Glock

hat this is the shortest chapter in the book is appropriate, because it's about the Model 18, the production Glock about which little is known and even less is seen.

To the casual observer, or someone viewing it only from the right side, the Model 18 can easily be mistaken for a Model 17. But it's not; no, it's definitely not.

The Model 18 Glock is a select-fire pistol capable of fully automatic firing at an incredibly high cycle rate—1,100 to 1,200 rounds per minute (RPM). That's an average of more than 19 rounds every second. At that rate the Model 18 can empty a 33-round magazine in only 1.72 seconds or a 19-round (9mm +2) magazine in just about one second!

Sure, it's a select-fire weapon; it can fire semi-automatically just like a standard Model 17. But there's something about that innocuous little lever, right where other manufacturers put their flip-flap safeties. You bet. There's something about that lever.

History

The Model 18 was first built in 1986 at the request of the Austrian antiterrorist Cobra Unit. They wanted a submachine gun that could be concealed easily under a coat, and Gaston Glock gave it to them. It was not imported into the United States until 1989.

As of this writing there were less than one hundred Model 18s in the United States, with various dignitary protection people in Washington, D.C., foreign embassies, and some tactical units of law enforcement departments. For the most part, however, Model 18s are sold in South America to police and other governmental agencies.

Differences between Models 17 and 18

The Model 18 may look very similar to the Model 17, but due to BATF requirements and Glock company policy, there are several significant differences:

1. Slide/frame rail dimensional differences. There are slight but significant dimensional differences in slide and frame rails between the Models 17 and 18. The Model 18's higher rails prevent its select-fire slide from being slipped onto a Model 17 receiver.
2. Other component dimensional differences. As many internal parts as practicable have been altered dimensionally so as to prevent someone from combining parts to make an unauthorized semi- or fully automatic Glock pistol, or "black market" Model 18. For example, the trigger bar group, the trigger mechanism housing, and the spacer sleeve are just different enough so that they're not interchangeable. That portion of the barrel—the outside of the chamber—that locks into the ejection port is unique to the Model 18.
3. Selector lever. That innocuous little lever on the rear of the slide, left side, that selects the firing mode: up (one dot) for semiautomatic fire, or down (two dots) for automatic fire. The selector switch

can be removed, making the pistol capable of semi-automatic fire only. The dots are merely subtle little dimples punched or stamped into the metal of the slide.

Selective-fire Glock Model 18, shown with standard-capacity magazine. Note that the slide-mounted firing mode selector lever is in up (one dot) position for semiautomatic firing.

4. Selector components. There are, in addition to the selector lever itself, three components necessary to permit the Model 18 to go full auto: 1) the selector lever plunger pin, 2) the selector lever plunger spring, and 3) the selector lever plunger spring bearing.

5. Barrels. Early Model 18s had barrels that were about 5 inches long, approximately 1/2 inch longer than the Model 17's barrel. Additionally, the longer Model 18 barrels had three lateral cuts in the top of that portion that extended outside in front of the slide. These cuts were essentially the same as those on the barrels of early Model 17Ls.

Barrel cuts, or ports, on the Model 18 were discontinued because the angle of cut caused combustion gasses to wreak havoc on front sights. All were blackened after a few magazines were fired, and some were even blown completely off the gun. According to factory personnel, allegations that ported barrels were discontinued on Model 18s because of cracking are untrue. (For more on this, see the Model 17L section in Chapter 6.)

Firing Characteristics

As mentioned previously, the Glock Model 18 cycles ammunition during automatic firing at between 1,100 and 1,200 RPM. This is about twice as fast as the Heckler & Koch MP5, the industry standard for law enforcement submachine guns.

Such a rapid cycle rate, coupled with its relatively small size for an automatic weapon, makes it a pistol for experienced operators. The familiar low bore axis, however, close to the operator's hand, common to all Glock pistols, compensates somewhat for the challenge of such a high cycle rate.

The Model 18 has no 3-round-burst trigger; none is available and none is contemplated. Competent automatic weapon operators know that technology can never replace quality training and that the best burst control is an educated and capable operator's trigger finger.

During extended firing, the barrel and slide can get rather hot—in fact, too hot to touch. The polymer frame, however, never gets hot, nor does the rear portion of the slide, so the operator needn't experience discomfort when manipulating the Model 18 during extended firing.

The Model 18 is, of course, a Glock; so, as with any Glock pistol, it is impervious to water. This is far more significant for the Model 18 than other Glock pistols because when it heats up during firing, one need only unload it, close the slide, and run it under water to cool it.

Glock Model 18 with 33-round magazine installed.

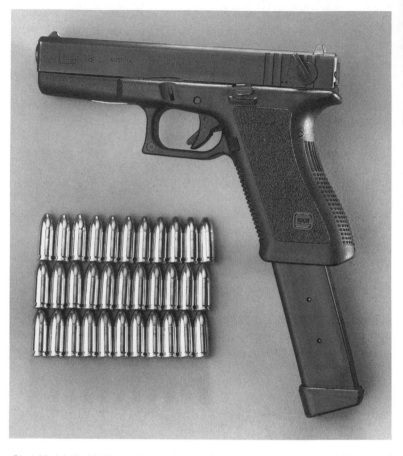

Glock Model 18 with 33-round magazine installed and 33 rounds of 9mm NATO ammunition.

• • • • •

The invisible Glock is as likely to remain virtually unseen in the future as it has been in the past. Unless and until federal statutes proscribing automatic weapons relax and Glock's policy restricting sales of the Model 18 to law enforcement customers changes (an unlikely combination of events, at least in the foreseeable future), most people will never see one.

Model 18: The Invisible Glock

Glock Model 18 with standard-capacity magazine installed, shown with 33-round magazine and 33 rounds of 9mm NATO ammunition.

CHAPTER 8

Models 22 and 23: The Fabulous Forties

aston Glock selected the number "17" for his first pistol because it was the seventeenth patent he received, the other sixteen being for designs of things other than firearms. As one would expect, especially from such an orderly man as Glock, the next pistol developed was the 17L, a long-slide version of the Model 17. Then came the Model 18 and soon after the Model 19.

A Little Confusion

Despite the orderliness, there was a little confusion about the Model 17's designation. Probably the most common misconception was the belief that it was called the "Glock 17" because the magazine held seventeen rounds. There's about as much truth to that as there is logic; the pistol could just have correctly been named the "Glock 18," had ammunition capacity been the origin of its designation.

About the time the Model 19 was introduced, Glock developed the ingenious "+2" magazine floorplates. These little marvels add a significant 2 rounds capacity to 9mm magazines, yet increase their size only a little bit. But as marvelous as these gadgets are, they did precipitate the confusion, which had nothing to do with the +2 floorplates themselves or how they functioned; it was something entirely different.

A Lot of Confusion

Original Model 17 magazines are 17-rounders, and standard Model 19 magazines are 15-rounders. When ordering, one needed only say, "Glock 17 or Glock 19 magazines, please," or "I'd like some Glock magazines, please; a couple of 17s and a couple of 15s."

But the advent of the Model 19 and the +2 floorplates brought befuddlement. "Give me a Glock 17 magazine" could mean one wanted an original Model 17 17-round magazine, a new +2 Model 17 19-round magazine, or a Model 19 +2 17-round magazine. And an innocuous "I'll take a Glock 19 magazine" could mean a standard 15-round Glock 19 magazine or a +2, 19-round magazine for the Model 17 or, in some cases, the Model 19.

People's jangled nerves were just beginning to calm in early 1990 when Glock Models 22 and 23 burst onto the scene. Some folks nearly broke down and cried with frustration, others wallowed in confusion, while still others put on a brave face and tried to pretend that they weren't baffled.

What were these strange Models 22 and 23? Where were the Models 20 and 21, and how come they (whatever they were) weren't here before the Models 22 and 23? Those really on the edge dared ask: "How many rounds will Model 22 and 23 magazines hold?" And, as if to add insult to injury, it soon came to light that not only did the new Models 22 and 23 appear to come before the Models 20 and 21 (whatever they were), but the 22 and 23 were evidently something bizarre called ".40 Smith & Wesson." Egad!

Unlike the confusion of the Models 17 and 19 pistols

and their various magazine combinations, there is some clarity to be achieved concerning the Models 22 and 23, why they seemed to precede the Models 20 and 21, and what the .40 Smith & Wesson business is all about.

History of the .40 Smith & Wesson Cartridge

This is a new ammunition cartridge that was developed jointly in 1989 by Winchester and Smith & Wesson, thus the S&W designation. It's not uncommon to name an ammunition cartridge after its developer. There are, for example, some named after Colt, the most well-known being the .45 ACP (Automatic Colt Pistol). As for Smith & Wesson, there are also several cartridges bearing its name, although the .40 S&W was the first for automatic pistols since the .35 Smith & Wesson in 1913.

The ".40" part of the .40 S&W cartridge comes, of course, from its caliber: .40 caliber equals 40/100 inch; it also equals 10mm. The .40 S&W could well have been called the "10mm Short," and, indeed, some people think of it as just that.

In the late 1980s the FBI was testing ammunition, seeking to replace its .357 revolvers with a tactically superior pistol. Eventually, the Smith & Wesson Model 1076 was selected, a 10mm pistol. John Hall, then chief of the bureau's Quantico, Virginia, Firearms Training Unit, liked the 10mm round but was concerned about two characteristics: 1) it produced a good deal of recoil, and 2) it was a bit flashy in low- or no-light situations.

A knowledgeable man and one of the few true wound ballistics experts in this country, Special Agent Hall knew that slightly downloading a powerful jacketed hollow-point (JHP) defense round would not diminish its potential for incapacitation. In fact, Hall was aware that sometimes reliability for incapacitating an assailant actually improves when a "hot" JHP round is slowed down a bit.

So Hall asked the folks at the Federal Cartridge

Company if they would supply some downloaded 10mm for evaluation purposes. They did, and Hall was pleased to note that the new round, quickly dubbed the "FBI Lite," was significantly milder in both recoil and muzzle flash yet performed just fine in ordnance gelatin and other viable testing media.

Shortly thereafter, in the summer of 1989, the FBI ordered 9,500 Smith & Wesson Model 1076s and 30 million rounds of Federal FBI Lite ammunition (180-grain Sierra JHP bullet in a standard 10mm case, downloaded to about 975 fps).

Left to right: a Winchester .40 Smith & Wesson 180-grain JHP cartridge (referred to by some as a 10mm Short), a 10mm Federal "FBI Lite" JHP cartridge, and a PMC 10mm 170-grain JHP cartridge.

While the above was transpiring, Smith & Wesson's president, Steve Melvin, thought, "If the FBI Lite round is downloaded, that means there's some airspace where there used to be gunpowder. That being the case, and considering the fact that there's only a silly millimeter difference between a '9' and a '10,' why not shorten the case length to the extent permitted by airspace and see if the shortened round can be stuffed into a 9mm-sized pistol?" Melvin approached Jerry Bersett, chief of the Olin Corporation's Winchester Ammunition Division, inquiring about the feasibility of his idea. It didn't take Winchester long to build the cartridge, essentially a "10mm Short." It was dubbed the .40 Smith & Wesson.

Right-side view of a Glock Model 22 prototype equipped with fixed sights. Note the absence of the third pin, which, on production models, is located just above and slightly to the rear of the trigger pin.

History of the Models 22 and 23

Smith & Wesson and Olin Winchester jointly introduced the .40 Smith & Wesson (the former its new Model 4006; the latter its new

.40 S&W cartridge) at the January 1990 SHOT show. It caused a significant stir. Shortly thereafter, Glock announced that it had two new pistols chambered for the .40 S&W cartridge.

Smith & Wesson built its Model 4006 based on the existing "Third Generation" Model 5906, a 9mm stainless steel pistol. Glock built the Models 22 and 23 based on its Models 17 and 19. Perhaps it had something to do with Glock pistols' elegant simplicity and astoundingly high percentage of interchangeable

parts, or perhaps it was something else. But in any case, Glock beat Smith & Wesson to the punch and got its .40-caliber pistols on the market first.

Right-side view of a Model 23 equipped with fixed sights.

Model Numbering Riddle Explained

The answer to the apparent nonsequential model numbering fuss is really quite simple. Before even becoming aware of the .40 S&W cartridge, Glock had decided to build two new pistols based on the same brand-new frame: the Model 20 in 10mm and the Model 21 in .45 ACP. While development was underway, however, Smith & Wesson and Olin Winchester announced the .40 S&W, and Glock realized it could build pistols chambered in that caliber based on already existing 9mm frames. Glock temporarily suspended development on the Models 20 and 21 and redirected its efforts to building two new .40-caliber pistols based on the Models 17 and 19 frames. As model numbers 20 and 21 were already assigned, the next two in sequence were 22 and 23. It is merely circumstance (and marketing wisdom) that Glock's Models 22 and 23 preceded its Models 20 and 21 (see Chapter 9) into production.

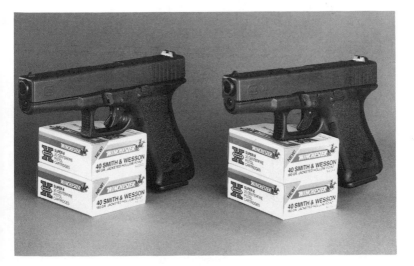

Glock Models 22 (left) and 23 (right), shown with boxes of Winchester .40 S&W ammunition.

The Fabulous Forties

Since their introduction in early 1990, the two .40-caliber Glock pistols have taken the firearms world by storm. By then the 9mm Models 17 and 19 had become so popular that any new pistol based on these models was certain to be successful. In fact, the 9mm Glocks were so well-liked that about the only improvement most delighted owners could have suggested would have been to build them in a larger caliber.

It's difficult to imagine a better decision for Glock to have made following the FBI's adoption of the 10mm "Lite" round than the one it did: to build its two incredibly popular pistols chambered for a new round that is ballistically equal to the FBI's 10mm ammunition while retaining everything else about the Models 17 and 19 that made them so popular.

Just about the only differences between the 9mm Model 17 and the .40-caliber Model 22 are: 1) the .40-caliber gun is .19 inch longer, and 2) it's .45 ounce heavier empty.

The smaller Models 19 and 23 pistols compare as follows: 1) the .40-caliber gun is .23 inch longer, and 2) it's actually .32 ounce lighter when empty.

There's not much else that can be said about Glock's forties, except, "fabulous."

CHAPTER 9

Glock's Big 10mm and .45 ACP Pistols

Model 20

n early 1989 the FBI was looking for a 10mm pistol that would become its official duty sidearm. Hoping to get in on the evaluation process, Glock developed a 10mm prototype in July of that year. It was the Model 20, the fifth pistol in Glock's stable, and it held great promise. But problems with test sample submissions and final FBI specifications made it impossible for the new pistol to participate in the tests.

Glock continued to develop the Model 20 through the remainder of 1989. But in January 1990, work on the 10mm pistol was suspended so the factory's developmental energies could be focused entirely on the Models 22 and 23.

In late summer 1990 work began again on the Model 20 project. The Model 20 was designed and developed to surpass the FBI's 40,000-round endurance specifications using full-power 10mm ammunition, not Federal's FBI "Lite" reduced-power loads. Glock also wanted to achieve maximum comfort and control in a full-power 10mm handgun.

Glock built 280 preproduction prototypes and sent them all to the United States for field testing. For nearly a year, law enforcement agencies and

sport shooters throughout the country tested
and evaluated the new 10mm pistol.

*Right-side view of a Glock Model 20 pro-
totype with fixed sights. Like other
Glock prototypes, this one
is missing the third
pin.*

Acceptance of
the Model 20 was re-
markable, perhaps because
it is the only Glock currently
produced that was devel-
oped specifically for the full-
power 10mm cartridge. The
Glock Model 20 was
designed from the start to
fire standard 10mm ammu-
nition. It is not a
redesigned pistol that orig-
inated from a .45 ACP performance concept, as were Colt's Delta
Elite, Smith & Wesson's 10XX series, and
virtually all other 10mm pistols on the market today.

In his January 1990 *Guns & Ammo* article, Wiley Clapp
states that the Glock Model 20 is ". . . a gun that fulfills the
promise made by the Bren 10 of a decade ago . . ."

Many people believe the ill-fated Bren Ten pistol and
the 10mm cartridge were developed contemporaneously.
Not so. The 10mm cartridge originally surfaced in 1972,
nine years before the Bren Ten pistol, as a wildcat. It was

called the .40 G&A (.40 caliber equals 10mm), and there was no gun to fire it in, so a Browning Hi-Power was converted from 9mm Parabellum to accommodate it.

The Bren Ten promise referred to by Wiley Clapp was for "a handgun of high capacity and modern features, shooting a completely new cartridge of markedly increased power." The Bren Ten (actually there were six models chambered for 10mm) might have fulfilled its vow had its manufacturer, a company called Dornaus & Dixon, not failed financially. About 1,500 pistols were built between 1983 and 1986, but even those were beset with problems.

If the Bren Ten might have been the high-capacity, modern handgun using the powerful 10mm cartridge that so many hoped for, how does Glock's Model 20 compare? Decide for yourself:

Feature	Bren Ten	Glock 20
Action Type	Double-Action Selective Double-Action	Glock "Safe Action" Double-Action Only
Capacity	11 + 1	15 + 1
Weight	29.25 oz.	26.35 oz.

The full-size Glock Model 20 comfortably handles full-power 10mm ammunition, but it also works well with the reduced-power Federal FBI "Lite" round. If overall size isn't a factor, the Model 20 offers users the dual capabilities of loading with FBI "Lite" ammunition for general defense purposes or using one of the several good-quality standard 10mm cartridges on the market appropriate for special defense situations, hunting, sport, or other purposes.

Model 21

Possibly the most ardently anticipated of all Glock

pistols was the .45 ACP Model 21. I recall hearing, not so many years ago, a few "experts"—mostly firearms trainers or former firearms trainers with one federal agency or another—pontificating about Glocks. Invariably during such discussions, someone would gripe about the fact that (in those days) Glock pistols were available only in 9mm Parabellum. "If only they'd build one in .45 ACP, I'd go for it in a minute," one expert would say. "You bet, but they never will," another would commiserate.

The general consensus between 1987 and 1988 was that Glock was selling so many Models 17 and 19 that it would never consider building one chambered for the venerable .45 ACP cartridge. "The R&D costs would outweigh potential profits," the experts said, "so why would they do it?"

A prototype Glock Model 21 with fixed sights, shown with two boxes of standard military-type 230-grain FMJ .45 ACP ammunition.

Glock's Big 10mm and .45 ACP Pistols

10mm Glock Model 20 (top) and .45 ACP Model 21 (bottom), both with fixed sights.

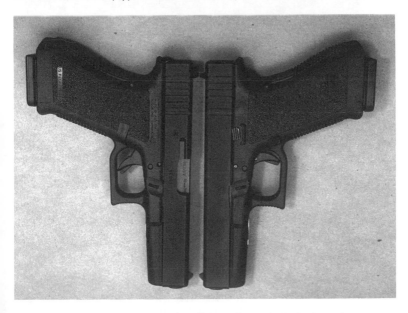

Model 20 (left) and Model 21 (right). Overall dimensions of both pistols are the same.

But despite the experts' doubts that it would ever produce a pistol chambered for .45 ACP, Glock announced that it intended to do just that.

Development of the Model 21 more or less paralleled that of the Model 20 for obvious reasons: both are built on the same frame, Glock's newest and largest receiver. In fact, the two big Glocks' physical specifications are identical except that the empty .45 ACP Model 21 is 1.13 ounces lighter than the empty 10mm Model 20. But the real issue regarding the bigger Models 20 and 21 isn't the difference between them; it's how much bigger they are in comparison to other Glocks.

Glock's Three Receivers

Top to bottom: small, medium, and large receivers compared.

The original Glock receiver used on the Models 17, 17L, 18, and 22, is now the midsize frame. The "compact" receiver used on the Models 19 and 23 differs only in that it's .24 inch shorter in height and .47 inch shorter in length. The height difference is entirely in the bottom of the handle, in the area of the magazine well. The length difference is entirely in that portion of the receiver forward of the trigger guard.

Size differences between the original Model 17 receiver and the new, larger, Model 20/21 receiver are of a broader scope than differences between Model 17 and Model 19 receivers. Height of the receivers of the midsize and large guns is the same, but length is not. The Model 17 is 7.21 inches long (Glock measures its pistol lengths at the slide), while the Models 20/21 are 7.44 inches long.

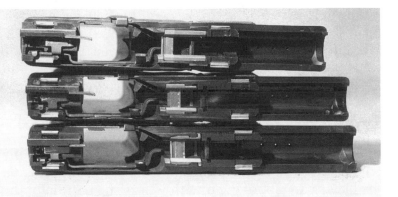

Comparison of Glock's three receivers from a different perspective.

NOTE: There are some significant discrepancies between dimensions shown in certain Glock literature and those actually measured on the pistols. In Glock's twelve-page pamphlet that includes specifications for Models 17, 17L, 19, 20, 21, 22, and 23, there is a typographical error in the height of the Model 21: it is shown as 6.16 inches; it should read 5.16 inches. But more curiously, all factory literature available for the Models 20 and 21 shows their overall (slide) length to be 8.27 inches. In reality, the overall length of the Models 20 and 21, measured at the slide, is 7.44 inches. That's a whopping .83 inch difference! (Glock offers no explanation for this, but it probably arose because the literature was printed before the prototypes were actually built and was based on original plans for the slide length, which changed somewhere along the way.)

Grip Size

Probably the most significant size increase in the new, larger Glock pistols—certainly the one most people express concern about—is grip size. One of the elements of grip size is width. The midsize receiver is 1.18 inches wide, an increase of .06 inch. And that's as far as Glock takes it—at least that's all the company's literature provides in the way of grip-related dimensions. But there are several components to grip size: 1) width, 2) length, and 3) circumference. As stated, the large receiver's grip is .06 inch wider than that of the midsize receiver. Likewise, the larger gun's grip is longer than that of the midsize gun. In fact, the former's is .13 inch longer at the base (mouth of the magazine well) and .18 inch longer at the point where the vertical serrations meet the stippling on the backstrap (about even with where the bottom of the trigger guard joins the frontstrap).

Of the dimensions that affect all the various factors of grip comfort/pistol controllability—the three dimensions listed above, plus such things as grip, frontstrap, and backstrap texture; grip shape; and recurve shape/placement—the most significant is undoubtedly circumference. After all, it's circumference that dictates hand placement on the pistol, and that, in turn, affects all those other factors. In the case of Glock's midsize receiver versus its large receiver, the latter is more than half an inch bigger around at the midpoint. Does that seem like a lot? Well, it depends upon how you look at it. The midsize frame's grip circumference is 5.88 inches at the midpoint, while the larger frame's is 6.44 inches. That's a difference of .56 inch, measured linearly. But circumference isn't effectively a linear measurement, so that can be deceiving. Viewed another way, the larger gun's circumference is less than 10 percent (.0952) greater than that of the midsize gun.

Is that a lot? Is it too much increase? Obviously, it's a subjective call. For some shooters who find the midsize grip acceptable, even very comfortable, the larger grip might be just fine; for others it may be unacceptably big.

From years of experience instructing with Glocks, I can unequivocally state that hand size versus grip size for handguns isn't as significant an issue as traditional gun lore would have it. We used to hear many complaints about the so-called overly large grips on the Glock Model 17. Now, however, such churlishness is seen only rarely, usually in malcontents who must find fault with everything or in hard-core traditionalists who refuse to admit that anything new can be good.

A Model 20 10mm Glock pistol in the hands of Peggi Bird of Threat Management Institute, just before she fired it for the first time.

Bird, firing a 10mm Glock Model 20, is an experienced large-caliber handgun shooter. This photo was taken just as the pistol was fired.

Here, Bird's pistol is partway through recoil. Note the ejected case just above the ejection port.

Bird's pistol has reached the highest point in its rise and is just beginning to start back down. The powerful 10mm cartridge produces significant muzzle rise, even in the relatively docile Glock Model 20 in the hands of a capable operator.

My hands aren't especially large, but I find absolutely no difficulty shooting the large-framed Glock pistols. The same is true for my partner, Peggi Bird, whose hands are significantly smaller than mine.

Two Final Differences

There are two additional small differences, one between the Model 21 and all other Glock pistols, and the other between the two large-frame guns and all the others.

The latter is noticeable only to the discerning: the magazine release on the two large-frame guns protrudes a teensy bit more than is normally the case on the medium- and small-framed ones. As you'll learn in Chapter 15, Glock makes an extended magazine catch. (The magazine catch is part #19 on the exploded diagram [p. 127], the tip of which is pressed by the shooter to release the magazine and is often called the magazine release.) By using this part in the wider grip of the new large receiver, Glock eliminated the need to make a third magazine catch—typical of the kind of Glock ingenuity that keeps things simple and inexpensive.

The extended magazine catch protrudes slightly more on the large-frame guns than the regular catch does on the midsize guns because the bigger gun is not as much wider than the midsize gun as the extended catch is longer than the regular catch.

Standard magazine catch with which all Models 17, 18, 19, 22, and 23 are shipped (left), and extended magazine catch used on Models 17L, 20, 21, and available as an option on the others (right).

Model 21 magazine (left) and Model 20 magazine (right). Note the indicator holes signify a capacity of only 13 rounds on the .45 ACP Model 21 magazine and 15 rounds on the 10mm Model 20 magazine.

The other difference—the one between the Model 21 and all other Glock pistols, including the Model 20—is that the Model 21's recoil spring and recoil-spring tube are an assembly, whereas on all other Glock pistols they are two separate parts. This is a great idea that is a welcomed modification to all other Glock pistols; it makes it much easier to reassemble the recoil spring and recoil-spring tube and fit them in place on the barrel and slide.

Muzzles of 10mm Model 20 (left) and .45 ACP Model 21 (right). Note the Model 21's different recoil spring tube—it's closed whereas all other models are open on the muzzle end.

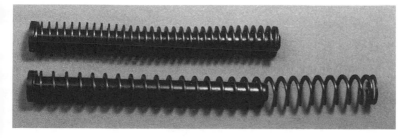

The integral recoil spring/tube assembly from a Model 21 (top) compared to a recoil spring and recoil spring tube as found in all other Glock pistols (bottom)

By the time you read this, all Glock pistols will be shipped with the recoil spring/recoil-spring tube assemblies instead of the two separate parts. Also, the assemblies will be available to retrofit earlier pistols if desired.

CHAPTER 10

Glock Pistols from the Inside Out

B y now you should have some concept, if you didn't before, of how truly remarkable Glock pistols are. You're about to find out exactly why.

I'm reminded of something I heard not long after acquiring my first Model 17, which was not long after Glock first came to the United States: "The least remarkable thing about the Glock pistol is that it's made of plastic."

I thought that a curious comment. After all, isn't the fact that they're made of plastic what they're all about? Hardly, but when all we've had B.G. (Before Glock) is a succession of guns that are all essentially variations on the same theme, it's understandable that when a refreshing new tune comes along we don't immediately recognize it for what it truly is.

Glock pistols are remarkable for many reasons, several of which are less obvious but just as (or more) significant as those that are well known. Thanks to the understandable ballistic naiveté just mentioned, coupled with the malignancy of the news media (see Chapter 2), the plastic thing comes to mind first, especially for those not so familiar with Glock pistols. Next most often thought of might be how comparatively few components they have, or that they "have no safety" (see Chapter 3, plus more below), or something about their enormous popularity in recent years.

The Glock table at the Raahaugee Shooting Sports Fair, just before the demonstration began. Note the eighteen disassembled Model 17s (two others are still in boxes at the far left corner of the table).

Component Count

Glock pistols have far fewer parts than are ordinarily found in other pistols. Company advertising claims Glock pistols have only thirty-three component parts, but this is somewhat misleading. As a matter of fact, it's flat-out wrong. For some reason, Glock counts each of two pairs of parts and one assembly as single components. The front and rear sights (16 and 16a on the exploded view), and the spring cups (8) are actually two parts each, but I suppose if one wishes to stretch the point each could be called a single component. The same would also

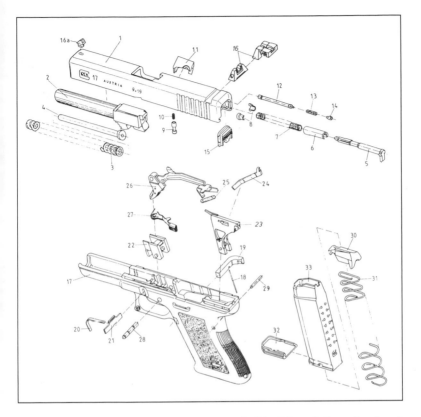

Exploded diagram of Glock pistol components: 1) slide, 2) barrel, 3) recoil spring, 4) recoil-spring tube, 5) firing pin, 6) spacer sleeve, 7) firing-pin spring, 8) spring cups, 9) firing-pin safety, 10) firing-pin safety spring, 11) extractor, 12) extractor depressor plunger, 13) extractor depressor plunger spring, 14) spring-loaded bearing, 15) slide cover plate, 16) rear sight, 17) receiver, 18) magazine catch spring, 19) magazine catch, 20) slide-lock spring, 21) slide lock, 22) locking block, 23) trigger mechanism housing with ejector, 24) connector, 25) trigger spring, 26) trigger with trigger bar, 27) slide-stop lever, 28) trigger pin, 29) trigger housing pin, 30) follower, 31) magazine spring, 32) magazine floor-plate, 33) magazine tube.

be true of the trigger with trigger bar (26), which is actually an assembly consisting of six parts (trigger bar, trigger, trigger safety, spring, and two pins) that aren't meant to be disassembled and can't be purchased separately.

This brings the total to thirty-five, if you (correctly) count the trigger and trigger bar assembly as a single component and the sights and spring cups as two parts each. Thirty-three, thirty-five . . . what's the difference, really, when you consider the fact that most pistols have far more parts? For example, a Colt Government Model can have from fifty-seven to nearly eighty parts (depending on the type, configuration, etc.), and some modern pistols have more still.

The thirty-five part count is the true total for only the 9mm pistols (Models 17, 17L, and 19); the .40-calibers (Models 22 and 23), the 10mm (Model 20), and the .45 ACP (Model 21) have an additional pin that brings their total number of parts to thirty-six. The Model 18 obviously has the selector lever on the left side of the slide that increases its parts count. In fact, there are three hidden components having to do with the selector lever and its ability to convert the Model 18 from a semiauto to a fully automatic pistol.

Slide Components

There are sixteen, seventeen, or eighteen (depending on how you count) components in a Glock pistol slide, including:

1. slide
2. barrel
3. recoil spring
4. recoil spring tube (guide rod)
5. front sight
6. rear sight
7. extractor
8. extractor depressor plunger
9. extractor depressor plunger spring
10. spring-loaded bearing
11. firing pin
12. spacer sleeve
13. firing pin spring

14. spring cups (2)
15. firing pin safety
16. firing pin safety spring
17. slide cover plate

NOTE: The above list excludes additional part(s) for the Model 18.

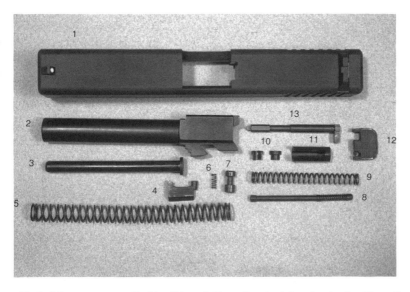

Glock slide components: 1) slide, 2) barrel, 3) recoil spring tube, 4) extractor, 5) recoil spring, 6) firing-pin safety spring, 7) firing-pin safety, 8) extractor depressor plunger, extractor depressor plunger spring, and the spring-loaded bearing (shown as an assembly), 9) firing-pin spring, 10) the spring cups, 11) spacer sleeve, 12) slide cover plate, and 13) firing pin.

Receiver Components

There are thirteen or fourteen (depending on the model) components in a Glock pistol receiver, including:

1. receiver, or frame
2. trigger with trigger bar
3. trigger spring

 4. trigger mechanism housing with (integral) ejector
 5. connector
 6. slide lock
 7. slide-lock spring
 8. magazine catch
 9. magazine-catch spring
10. slide-stop lever
11. locking block
12. trigger pin
13. trigger housing pin
14. locking block pin (on Models 20, 21, 22, and 23 only)

Glock receiver components: 1) locking block, 2) slide-lock spring, 3) trigger pin, 4) slide lock, 5) trigger with trigger bar assembly, shown here mated with the trigger mechanism housing with ejector (the small projection from the trigger mechanism housing directly above the trigger bar and below the trigger guard), 6) trigger housing pin, 7) slide-stop lever; and 8) magazine catch.

Magazine Components

There are four magazine components, any way you count them:

1. magazine tube (body, shell, etc.)
2. magazine follower
3. magazine spring
4. magazine floorplate

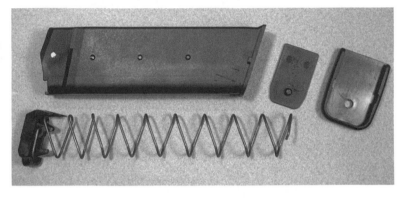

Glock magazine components. Left to right, top: magazine tube, subfloorplate, floorplate. Bottom: magazine spring with follower in place. NOTE: 9mm magazines do not have the subfloorplate; pictured here is a Model 21 .45 ACP magazine.

Component Interchangeability among Pistols

One of the many remarkable things about Glock pistols is that all parts are fully interchangeable among guns of the same model. This means that you can disassemble several pistols of the same model, mix up their parts, and reassemble the same number of guns indiscriminately using parts from all the different original ones.

In fact, just such a thing was done. In May 1990, at the Raahaugee Shooting Sports Fair in Ontario, California, members of the California Rangemasters Association fired 10,140 rounds of Federal 9mm Parabellum ammunition in a rather unique Glock pistol.

Twenty Glock Model 17s were completely disassembled. All their parts were then mixed up so it was impossible to determine which parts had been together in which pistols originally. Someone grabbed a receiver, serial number MU421US, and then all the other parts necessary to assemble one complete Model 17 were taken at random from the various piles.

Following assembly and function checks, magazines were loaded, and the firing began. Three hours and forty-seven minutes later, 10,140 rounds had been fired. During that period the pistol was fieldstripped and the breechface and chamber were cleaned every 2,500 rounds. Also during the three hours and forty-seven minutes, mandatory range cease-fires (remember, the testers were all rangemasters) for target changes were accomplished.

The pistol malfunctioned once: at 4,500 rounds a trigger spring ($1.95) broke. Another was grabbed from the mixed-up parts pile and installed in less than one minute, and the firing resumed. (By the way, if you wonder about installing that trigger spring in less than a minute, it isn't a typo or an exaggeration. Not long before writing this, during a Glock Police Service Division Armorer's Course at the California Department of Justice Training Center in Sacramento, I restored to full functionality a completely disassembled—not merely fieldstripped, I mean taken down to the very last component—Model 17 in one minute and twenty-one seconds during a timed check. It's no big deal to put one back together in under two minutes, or partially disassemble one and change something such as a trigger spring, then reassemble it in one minute.)

Component Interchangeability between Models

One of the many amazing things about Glock pistols is that so many parts are interchangeable between various models. For example, between the Model 17 and Model 19, only ten parts do not interchange:

1. slide
2. barrel

3. recoil spring
4. recoil-spring tube
5. receiver
6. slide-lock spring
7. locking block
8. slide-stop lever
9. magazine spring
10. magazine tube

NOTE: Beginning with serial number EH000, trigger with trigger bar assemblies became interchangeable between Models 17 and 19. For pistols older than serial number EH000, trigger with trigger bar assemblies are not interchangeable.

Because the .40-caliber Model 22 is very similar to the 9mm Model 17 (the only differences being those necessary to accommodate the Model 22's larger caliber), and because the .40-caliber Model 23 is likewise very similar to the 9mm Model 19, the parts interchangeability situation between the two pairs of pistols is correspondingly similar.

Recoil spring tube with recoil spring in place for the Model 23 (top) and the Model 19 (bottom).

The differences between the 9mm and .40-caliber pistols, due to larger caliber in the latter, include such items as:

1. a third pin situated through the locking block just above and slightly ahead of the trigger pin
2. a stronger recoil spring and recoil spring tube

3. a .40-caliber barrel
4. a .40-caliber magazine follower

Recoil springs removed from the guide rods. Note that the .40-caliber Model 23's rod (top) is smaller in diameter to accommodate the larger, more powerful spring required.

The aft end of a recoil spring tube and spring assembly for a 9mm pistol in place. Note how the large end of the tube fits into the semicircular lower step in the forward barrel lug.

Just as parts commonalities and differences exist between the larger-framed Models 17 and 22 on the one hand and the smaller-framed Models 19 and 23 on the other hand, and just as there are other differences and similarities due to caliber between the 9mm and .40-caliber pistols, likewise are there both kinds of crossovers and inconsistencies between the 10mm Model 20 and the .45 ACP Model 21.

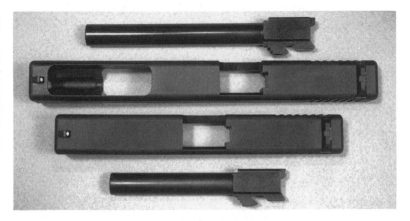

The only noninterchangeable parts between Models 17 and 17L. Top to bottom: Model 17L barrel, Model 17L slide, Model 17 slide, and Model 17 barrel. Note the large cutout in the top of the Model 17L slide.

Between the Model 17 and the competition Model 17L, only the slide and barrels do not interchange. This means that someone can have the Model 17L's long slide and barrel plus a complete Model 17 and actually have two guns. Because Glocks are so quick and easy to work on, conversion from one to the other can be accomplished in minutes. (Differences between the Model 17 and Model 18 are covered in Chapter 7, "Model 18: The Invisible Glock.")

Polymer Components

As discussed above, and more thoroughly in Chapter 2, which details the Jack Anderson/news media fiasco, the fact that Glocks are made of plastic is probably the most widely known thing about them. That Gaston Glock makes his pistols using a good deal of polymer is important and should not be minimized or ignored. Neither should more be made of it than is appropriate.

Actually, Glock pistols are 83-percent steel and only 17-percent polymer by weight. The polymer is Polymer 2, invented by Glock himself. It is a specially formulated plastic that contains ingredients to increase durability.

Polymer 2 is used for the receiver (frame) and other internal parts. Some, such as the recoil-spring tube (guide rod), the slide cover plate, spacer sleeve, spring-loaded bearing, and spring cups, are components of the slide. Others, such as the magazine catch, trigger-mechanism housing (but not the integral ejector), trigger, trigger safety, and, of course, the receiver itself, are receiver components. The magazine is entirely polymer except for the spring and inserts.

Polymer 2 is more resilient and stronger than carbon steel and steel alloys. They will warp and tend to become brittle at temperature extremes, but Polymer 2 won't. Polymer 2 resists heat up to 392°F and cold down to -75°F. Glock pistols must pass functional firing tests at temperatures ranging from +140°F to -40°F.

Metal Components

As extraordinary as Polymer 2 is, the metal used in Glock pistols is equally so. Nearly all metal parts in Glock pistols are coated with an exceptionally hard finish. The exceptions are the slide stop, trigger bar, extractor, extractor depressor plunger, ejector, and slide lock, which are Parkerized (bonded finish); the frame rails, which are chrome steel; and the springs, which are unfinished spring steel.

All other metal parts, including the slide and the inside and outside of the barrel, are coated with a finish called Tenifer. Tenifer is applied in a 500°C (932°F) nitrate bath to give the coated parts a skin hardness of 69 Rockwell Cone (RC). This is extremely hard; by comparison, a metal file's hardness is only 62 to 65 RC, and the hardness of an industrial diamond is 70 RC.

Glock's Tenifer coating penetrates the metal so that coated parts have a hardness of 55 to 60 RC at a depth of .02mm (.05 inch) below the surface. From 20 to 30 percent deeper, the hardness is still 48 to 50 RC. Metal this hard is incredibly durable.

Glock pistols' Tenifer-coated parts are 99-percent saltwater-corrosion resistant and proved superior to stainless steel in seven-day saltwater pitting tests. Tenifer meets or exceeds all stainless steel specifications; stainless steel is softer due to added alloys.

The highly salt-resistant polymer components and Tenifer-coated steel parts are especially important to people who carry their Glocks on their person, and especially directly next to their body. Glock pistols' high degree of salt-resistance enables them to better endure the harmful effects of perspiration, making them more reliable and easier to maintain than other guns. Likewise, Glocks are virtually impervious to the myriad of airborne contaminants so increasingly prevalent in industrialized and urban areas.

Glock pistols, with their Tenifer-coated metal and polymer parts, are also more corrosion-resistant than guns with any other finish, coating, or material currently available, including all the various applications of hard chrome plating, phosphates, Teflon, blueing, stainless steel, and other alloys.

Barrel

The barrels of most pistols have "square" rifling (i.e, grooves) cut into the barrel walls. But rifling in the barrels of Glock pistols is hammer-forged. Here's the difference: In barrels with conventional rifling, square grooves are cut into the barrel by a broaching machine that runs through the bore. It rotates when passing through to produce the desired "twist" in the rifling.

Glock's technique involves beating a mandril through the bore to produce a hexagonal shape. There are no lands and grooves in the conventional sense. All Glock pistol barrels have hexagonal rifling (six "grooves"), except the .45-caliber Model 21, which has octagonal rifling (eight "grooves"). The length of twist varies slightly among the calibers: 9mm barrels on Models 17, 17L, and 19 are 9.84 inches; .40-caliber barrels on Models 22 and 23 are 15.75 inches; the 10mm barrel on the Model 20 and the .45 ACP barrel on the Model 21 are both 15.75 inches. The length of twist is the distance required for a bullet to make one full (360-degree) revolution.

Barrels with square-cut rifling are somewhat weaker because some of the metal has been removed by the cutting process; thus, the barrel wall thickness in the area of each groove is diminished. Glock barrels, instead of being slightly weaker at the rifling points, actually are molecularly more dense in the six rifling areas.

Another advantage of Glock barrels is that the bores are slightly smaller than conventional barrels of the same caliber. On conventional pistols, 9mm bores are usually .357 to .360 caliber (inches), but the Glock's 9mm bore is .356 caliber. This produces a better gas seal, meaning that significantly more combustion gasses are trapped behind the bullet as it is expelled from the casing and moves down the bore, slightly increasing velocity and stability and improving pistol function. It also makes Glocks shoot slightly harder, all else being equal. But all else isn't equal when Glocks are compared to conventional pistols. See discussions of ergonomics and felt recoil in Chapter 13, "Design Features," for more on this subject.

Safeties

As we've discussed previously, Glock engenders considerable comment and controversy in connection with its approach to safeties. We know that those who do not like or do not understand Glock pistols decry the "absence" of safeties, or at least the absence of an affirmative safety.

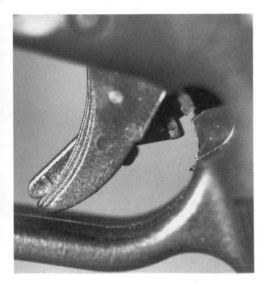

Glock's controversial trigger safety. The small device that protrudes from the trigger's face is actually only the forward part of the trigger safety. The latter part extends behind the trigger; the entire device pivots on the steel pin seen here near the top of the trigger. The trigger safety's squared rear face is stopped by the frame, thereby preventing rearward trigger movement until the shooter's finger pushes the forward-protruding part flush with trigger face, pivoting the rear corner up, allowing it to clear the frame, and permitting full rearward trigger movement.

The argument over the pistol's lack of an affirmative safety will likely endure for some time. Those with views rooted in tradition, purists, and people who follow the lead of doomsayers (and others convinced that the only acceptable way to keep people from unintentionally discharging their pistols is to equip them with devices that must be deactivated before the gun will fire) are unlikely to ever be entirely comfortable with Glock pistols.

On the other hand, well-trained people confident in their own abilities and those of others similarly competent will have no problem embracing Glock pistols as safe. The fundamental elements of such confidence are: 1) theoretical training leading to a thorough understanding of the system, which is foundational for 2) practical training in the safe and effective application of the system.

Glock pistols have three separate safeties, as follows:

1. The *trigger safety* eliminates the possibility of unintentionally discharging the pistol unless and until it is fully depressed.

2. The *firing pin safety* positively blocks the firing pin from moving forward, thus eliminating the possibility of firing a cartridge that might be in the chamber, unless and until the trigger is pulled all the way to the rear.

Glock's firing-pin safety is actually comprised of two parts: a small, multi-diameter pin and a tiny spring.

The firing-pin safety spring fits into a hollow portion of the larger end of the firing-pin safety itself.

The firing-pin safety assembly ready for installation in the slide.

The firing-pin safety assembly installed in the slide. Careful examination shows that the firing pin cannot move forward (left in the photograph) when the firing pin safety is in this position, i.e., when the trigger has not been moved to the rear. Rearward trigger movement causes the upward-projecting tab to move the firing pin safety upward, thereby bringing the smaller-diameter portion of the safety adjacent to the firing pin, allowing the firing pin to move forward past the safety.

3. The *drop safety* prevents unintentional discharge if the pistol is dropped.

The theory behind the design of these three safeties, and how each one works, is explained in Chapter 11.

Firing Mechanism

Glock pistols do not have the conventional sear/hammer arrangement so often found in semiautomatics. In fact, Glock pistols have no hammer at all. Instead, they have what some people refer to as a "striker," but what others simply call the firing pin.

Trigger mechanism housing with ejector. Muzzle direction is toward the left, the way the ejector (top left corner) is facing. The round hole through the bottom of the housing accommodates the trigger housing pin. The flat metal piece in the rectangular cutout (at about the seven o' clock position from the inverted numeral 2) is the end of the connector that lies flush against the housing on the other side. The connector runs toward the upper right of the housing and ends just behind the New York trigger spring, a portion (the angled straight piece with the rounded tip) of which can be seen through the drop safety cutout (the bi-level polygon near the top of the housing).

Since pistols were first conceived of, the device that caught and held the hammer against the mainspring and released it when pulled away has been called the sear. Most sears rather look alike because most pistols are very similar in design, although occasionally one runs across a weird one (sear or pistol, take your pick). Using the above definition for sear, I suppose what Glock pistols have, both to hold and to release the striker (firing pin), should be called a sear. But because they (Glocks or what Glock pistols have, take your pick) are so unconventional, it seems somehow wrong to label them such, although the factory does sometimes refer to the part in question as a "sear plate."

The firing mechanism of Glock pistols is, like everything else about them, very simple and straightforward. Conventional sear/hammer arrangements with all their springs, pins, linkage, and various apparatuses are replaced by this thing (the sear plate, if you must) that is an integral part of the trigger bar. That's it. No hammer, no mainspring, no myriad of cranky, interdependent parts; no need.

A complete explanation of how the Glock pistol's firing mechanism functions follows in Chapter 11.

The rear portion of the trigger bar (left) with the cruciform sear plate clearly identifiable and the trigger mechanism housing with ejector (right). The left wing (pointing downward in this photograph) of the sear plate projects into the drop safety cutout when the two assemblies are mated.

Here the trigger bar has been mated with the trigger mechanism housing (lying on its left side). The left wing of the sear plate can be seen extending into the drop safety cutout.

The left wing of the sear plate in the drop safety cutout. Here the trigger is in the forward position; the left wing of the sear plate is in the forward, or upper, portion of the cutout, thus preventing the sear plate/trigger bar from dropping below the downward-projecting tang of the firing pin, thereby releasing the firing pin.

Another view of the sear plate/trigger mechanism housing relationship in the trigger-forward position.

143

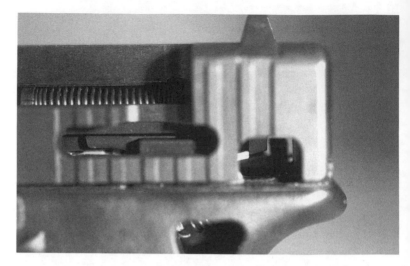

The rear slide area of the cutaway Model 19 reveals much of Glock's elegantly simple firing mechanism: the firing-pin spring, retained by the spring cups, is visible in the large cutout in the upper left portion of the photograph. Below that, in the long rectangular cutout with rounded ends, the upper left portion of the trigger mechanism housing and the ejector can be seen. Behind that, in the cutout directly below the rear sight, is a glimpse of the downward-projecting firing-pin tang restrained by the rear wing of the sear plate. As the trigger is moved to the rear, the firing-pin spring compresses further, the sear plate moves down in the drop safety's bi-level cutout, and the firing pin is released to move forward.

Here, the trigger has been moved to the rear, causing the rear tab of the trigger bar to slide down the connector's angled ramp; the bi-level drop safety cutout has allowed the sear plate to drop down, releasing the firing pin and allowing it to move forward to fire a chambered round of ammunition.

144

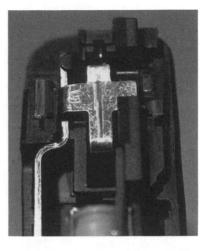

Here's what the trigger-to-the-rear condition looks like when the assemblies are installed in the receiver (above).

Another view of the sear plate/trigger mechanism housing relationship, this time in the trigger-to-the-rear position (above left).

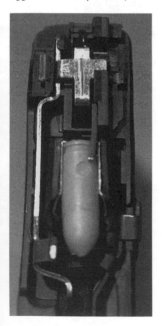

Another trigger-to-the rear view; in this one almost the entire trigger can be seen. The upward-projecting trigger-bar tab is just to the right (above in the photo) of the plastic training ammunition round. The ejector can be seen partially extending over the ammunition round in the magazine, held there by the metal lips on either side.

Sights

Glock pistols are available with three types of sight systems:

1. standard fixed sights, supplied with a squared, U-shaped white outline on a fixed rear sight blade and a white dot on the front post-type sight.
2. adjustable sights, supplied with a squared, U-shaped white outline on an elevation-adjustable rear sight and a white dot on the front post-type sight.
3. night sights, supplied with two tritium dots on a fixed rear sight blade and a tritium dot on the front post-type sight.

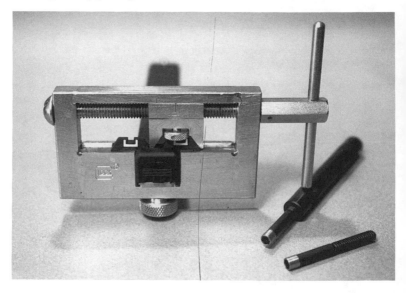

The Glock sight installation tools. The rear sight installation device is shown with a slide in place, one fixed rear sight (left) being replaced with another (right). The rear sight tool's T-handle is resting on the special tool Glock makes for night sight installation; the installed socket is for Trijicon sights and the other is for Meprolights.

The standard (fixed and adjustable) rear sights and the

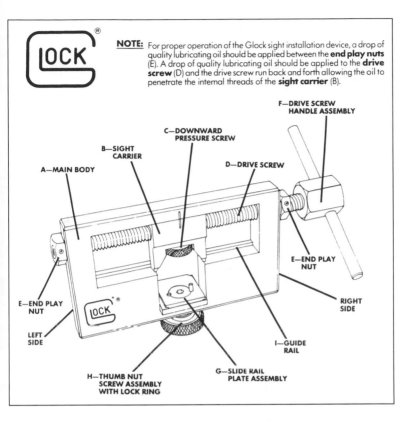

NOTE: For proper operation of the Glock sight installation device, a drop of quality lubricating oil should be applied between the **end play nuts** (E). A drop of quality lubricating oil should be applied to the **drive screw** (D) and the drive screw run back and forth allowing the oil to penetrate the internal threads of the **sight carrier** (B).

Part of a page from Glock's sight installation device instructional procedures.

standard front sight are polymer. The night sights are metal. Front sight height is .160 inch (4mm). Fixed rear sights are available in four different heights. The standard sight is .260 inch (6.5mm) and is marked only with a single line on the right side.

The one fixed rear sight that is lower than standard (used to lower target impact point) is .244 inch (6.1mm) and is marked with a long line above a short line on the right-hand side of the sight.

The two fixed rear sights that are higher than standard (used to raise target impact point) are .276 inch (6.9mm) and .291 inch (7.3mm), respectively. They are marked with one short line above a long line and two short lines above a long line, respectively.

All rear sights are dove-tailed in place and are drift-adjustable for lateral correction. Glock makes a nifty rear sight installation tool that can also be used for lateral adjustment of rear sights.

A closer look at the rear sight installation process. The sight carrier pushes the installed sight out of the dovetail while simultaneously installing the new one. The slide is held in place by the slide rail plate assembly (just below the slide cover plate). The slide is positioned laterally by the plate engaging the slide rails (seen here), and longitudinally by an upward-protruding pin in the assembly that contacts the camming cut in the right-side slide rail.

Night sights are relatively new for firearms, having been introduced in the mid-1980s. They are tiny vials of tritium, a radioactive substance that emits a greenish light, the use of which is controlled by the Nuclear Regulatory Commission (NRC). According to NRC regulations, the actual vials can be handled only by those licensed by the NRC. Once the vials are encapsulated in modules and the modules are installed in gun sights, the sights can be handled by anyone.

Glock offers night sights from two different sources: Hesco (LaGrange, Georgia) and Armson (Farmington, Michigan). Hesco's product is made in Israel and marketed throughout North America as Meprolights. Armson actually manufacturers its product and markets it worldwide under the name Trijicon.

Of course, both Hesco and Armson claim product superiority, but with something where visual impression is so important, specifications and technical differences often mean less than what users see and feel about the products. Each company claims its night sights are better than the other's in various ways, the most obvious being brightness. But actual light emission isn't all there is to good night sights.

Night sights have to be used in daylight too, and how they appear when it's too bright to see the green glow of tritium is important. Both companies deal with this problem by outlining the tritium modules with white substances that make the sights appear much the same as standard three-dot sight systems.

Again, total light emission isn't the only criterion of significance for use in darkness. Sharpness is also important, and here there is a difference between Meprolights and Trijicon night sights.

Meprolights are entirely encapsulated in a patented synthetic bonding substance that completely seals the tritium vial and makes it impervious to gun cleaning solvents. Hesco makes no disclaimers regarding this and says Meprolights can be fully immersed in these products without risk of damage.

Trijicon night sights are encased in a canister that has a patented industrial sapphire lens that covers that portion of the tritium seen by the shooter. Armson says its Trijicon night sights can be immersed safely in any conventional gun cleaning product, but it warns against prolonged immersion in acetone- or ethanol-based products (although such products can be wiped or swabbed on briefly for cleaning without harm).

Neither type of night sight should be immersed in products containing trichloride compounds, such as 111 Trichlorethane used in Prolix, although Armson states that, as with the acetone- and ethanol-based products, brief exposure to trichloride compounds through wiping or swabbing won't hurt Trijicon sights.

The gluelike substance used to encapsulate Meprolights may make them somewhat more invasion-resistant than Trijicon sights, but it also diffuses emitted light, whereas Armson's sapphire lenses don't. Crisp, clear green dots can be advantageous on night sights; one federal agency that comparison-tested the two products reported their agents fired shot groups one-third tighter with Trijicon night sights than with Meprolights.

Glock sells both products for the same price and says that they're about equally popular. Some firearms products wholesalers, however, sell Meprolights for significantly less than Trijicon sights.

Other Features

There are many other remarkable features of Glock pistols, most (if not all) of which are described elsewhere in this book including (but not limited to) Chapter 11, "How Glock Pistols Function," and Chapter 14, "Glock Accessories and Special Stuff." See also the "New York Trigger Spring" section of Chapter 3, "The Law Enforcement Phenomenon."

How Glock Pistols Function

lock pistols are recoil operated, double-action-only semiautomatics (except for the selective-fire Model 18, which can fire fully automatically). Glocks use a locking system similar to the ubiquitous Colt/Browning tilting barrel type (the breech, or chamber, end of the barrel tilts down to unlock it from the slide after firing). The actual lock-up (the manner in which a pistol's barrel is firmly held in position when the gun is in the ready-to-fire configuration, and also when a cartridge is actually discharged) is more in the style of SIG-Sauer (the barrel hood above the chamber enters the ejection port to form a solid lock against the breechface).

Recoil-Operated Pistols

The action of recoil-operated pistols is powered by the rearward component of force generated by the fired ammunition cartridge. Essentially, this rearward force is the physical reaction, à la Newton's Second Law of Motion (commonly stated as: "For every action there is an equal and opposite reaction"), to the force that motivates the bullet down the barrel, out the muzzle, and on to the target.

While recoil-operated semiautos are quite common, probably the most familiar of them is the famous Browning-designed Colt Government Model (1911) design. Old John Moses was truly a genius as firearms designers go, but his design is a bit complicated, especially with regard to the lock-up. Several more modern pistols have improved lock-up designs that are simpler but function just as well or better than the 1911-type. Glock's design is one of the best.

1911-Type Locking/Lock-Up

Barrels of pistols with 1911-type actions are frequently attached to the frame by a pin-and-lever (called a slide stop), the pin portion of which runs laterally through attach points on the frame and an oval-shaped link on the underside of the barrel, just below the chamber. The link is attached to the barrel by a pin that allows the link, sometimes called a "swinging link," to pivot, or swing, fore and aft.

If set in position on the frame without the slide but attached by the slide stop, the barrel can pitch slightly muzzle-up and muzzle-down because nothing other than the slide-stop pin affixes it to the frame, and nothing restrains it from rocking up and down a bit. But when fully assembled with the slide in place and all the way forward ("in battery"), the muzzle is forced into a tight-fitting sleeve (called a barrel bushing) at the front of the slide. This bushing holds the muzzle firmly in position and prevents the barrel from pitching or otherwise moving about.

Additionally, when the pistol is fully assembled and in battery, two ribs (barrel lugs) projecting upward from the top of the barrel mate with two recesses milled in the underside of the slide top. While this symbiotic mating has nothing to do with accuracy, as does the barrel bushing, it is nevertheless very important.

How Glock Pistols Function

Firing Cycle: 1911-Style

At the moment of firing, recoil force starts the slide moving to the rear. The barrel lugs (mated with the slide recesses) cause the barrel to move straight back with the slide. It's important that the barrel remain firmly affixed to the slide until the bullet exits the muzzle, or accuracy goes down the tubes. As the slide/barrel assembly reaches a certain point of rearward travel, the swinging link pivots so as to pull the breech end of the barrel downward. This causes the barrel lugs to drop clear of the slide recesses, referred to as unlocking the barrel from the slide. When the barrel is unlocked from the slide, the slide continues rearward without it.

During all this time the extractor has been removing the fired casing from the firing chamber. After a bit more rearward travel, the ejector will "kick" the empty casing out through the ejection port. Shortly thereafter the slide will reach the rearmost extent of its travel, at which point the recoil spring (which was being compressed during rearward movement of the slide) takes over and moves the slide forward into battery.

Glock Locking/Lock-Up

Glock barrels (#2 on the exploded diagram, p. 127) have no swinging link, and they're not attached to the receiver (#17, frame) by a pin or any other such device. Also, Glock barrels aren't restrained at the muzzle end by a bushing or anything else. Glock accuracy, barrel/slide locking, and many other features, are accomplished quite differently from the traditional Colt/Browning types and their progeny.

On the underside of Glock pistol barrels, beneath the chamber, are two projections, i.e., barrel lugs. These are integral with the barrel/chamber; in fact, the whole thing (barrel/chamber/lugs) is machined from one solid block of steel. The two lugs are "slanted" to the rear; their fore and aft surfaces are cut at about a forty-five-degree angle down and back from the underside of the chamber.

The rear face of the back lug, actually the feed ramp, is milled so it's slightly concave to guide the nose of the cartridge up and into the chamber. The front face of the back lug is a flat surface that angles back slightly more than the feed ramp.

The front lug is about 1/4 inch forward of the back lug. Its rear face is angled back about parallel to the front face of the back lug, but at first glance it appears to be otherwise due to the odd angle at which the roughly 1/4 inch of flat chamber underside is cut. The front face of the front lug is multifaceted, with a couple of "steps" milled into it. The first step has a semicircular recess to accommodate the large end of the recoil-spring tube (guide rod). The face of the other step is a squared channel running crosswise so that the extreme lower part forms a "lip" that is vital to proper functioning.

When the pistol is fully assembled and in battery, the slide (1) is prevented from coming forward off the receiver by the lip on the front face of the front barrel lug catching in a corresponding groove on the rear face of the slide lock (21). The slide lock is a flat piece of metal running across the receiver just above and slightly forward of the trigger (26). The ends of the slide lock are pulled down for slide/receiver disassembly (many people mistakenly believe these two ends to be two unconnected parts). Forward pressure is applied to the slide by the recoil spring (3), keeping the barrel lug pressed against the slide lock.

When in battery, part of the locking block (22) projects upward just behind the front lug. This portion of the locking block sits about 1/16 inch behind the rear face of the front barrel lug; their respective angles match. The upward-projecting part of the locking block also is about 1/16 inch higher than the bottom of the front lug but is slightly lower than the rear barrel lug, which doesn't hang down as far as the front one. The upward-projecting part of the locking block is sized to fit nicely into the space between the two barrel lugs.

To form the actual lock-up—to maintain the barrel's position relative to the slide at the moment of and briefly after discharge—the upper rear face of the chamber is snug against the breechface. When held by rearward pressure on the front barrel lug, countered by forward pressure exerted on the back of the upper chamber by the breechface, the barrel is firmly locked in place.

Firing Cycle: Glock-Style

When a cartridge in the chamber is fired, recoil force starts moving the slide/barrel assembly to the rear. When the assembly has traveled rearward about 1/16 inch, the rear face of the front barrel lug contacts the front of the upward-projecting portion of the locking block. At this point, sufficient time has elapsed for the bullet to travel down the bore and exit the muzzle, so barrel lock-up is no longer necessary.

In this cutaway view, the barrel lugs can be seen in relation to the locking block, which is just above the trigger pin, just below the rear barrel lug, and behind the front barrel lug. The large end of the recoil spring tube can be seen in place in the semicircular step of the forward barrel lug. The upward-projecting arm of the trigger bar is just behind the rear barrel lug.

Continued rearward progression of the slide/barrel assembly causes the rear face of the front barrel lug to slide down the front of the locking block due to the angle at which they are cut. In turn, the entire rear portion of the barrel drops down, unlocking it from the slide. When the rear of the barrel has dropped about 3/16 inch, there is sufficient clearance for the top of the slide to pass over the chamber, thus permitting the slide to continue to its rearmost extreme without the barrel.

As with other pistols, case extraction, case ejection, and fresh cartridge feeding into the chamber all occur during slide cycling. As the slide goes into battery, the unlocking sequence is reversed: the upper portion of the breechface contacts the upper rear face of the chamber, pushing it forward. The front face of the rear barrel lug pushes against and slides up the rear portion of the upward-projecting part of the locking block, causing the rear of the barrel to rise and lock up with the slide.

Glock Locking/Lock-Up Advantages

1911-types and others that utilize links and pins to retain the slide on the frame often require tools (or at the very least many fingers and much fingertip pressure) to remove slide from frame. Glock's design permits slide removal without tools. Moreover, it can be accomplished easily and unbelievably fast.

Other modern designs, such as those of SIG-Sauers and Berettas, permit slide removal without tools, but none is as easy, fast, or safe as that of the Glock. And Glock pistols cannot have their slides removed at inauspicious times by criminals on the street as Beretta 92Fs and M9s can. (But then, Beretta is an innovator in the area of multiple methods of slide removal, e.g., the rearward separation of slide from frame during firing on M9 slides containing tellurium.)

Conventional Pistol Cocking Function

Conventional single-action and selective-action semi-autos are cocked by rearward travel of the slide. Usually a portion of the slide, often the rear face, pushes against the front face of the hammer, cocking the hammer and allowing the slide to pass over it on its way to the rear.

NOTE: Do not confuse "selective-action" with "selective-fire." The former refers to a pistol that can be fired in the single-action mode after hammer-cocking, or that can be "decocked" from single-action mode to double-action mode using a decocking lever. The latter refers to a firearm that can be switched (selected) between fully automatic operation and semiautomatic operation using a selector switch installed on the gun.

Double-action-only pistols completely bypass hammer-cocking when the slide cycles. These pistols can be cocked only with the trigger, using internal mechanisms that function much like those in the old police-type revolvers.

Conventional Pistol Hammer-Sear Design

Conventional pistol hammers are spring-loaded to the forward position by a mainspring located in the rear portion of the grip, behind the magazine well. The lower portion of the hammer is circular-shaped with (usually) two notches on the front side. These two notches are engaged by the nose of the sear, a part (usually) located behind the magazine well inside the pistol's grip. The sear is also spring-loaded (nose to the rear) by its own spring, also located inside the grip behind the magazine well.

The upper trigger notch is the half-cock notch; the lower is the full-cock notch. When the hammer is cocked, the sear catches in one or the other of these notches, usually the full-cock notch. The sear's nose, spring-loaded rearward against the forward spring-loading of the hammer, catches in the notch and prevents the hammer from falling. At this point the gun is cocked. Pulling the trigger activates internal mechanisms that pull the sear's nose out of the notch and permit the spring-loaded hammer to "fall" and hit the firing pin.

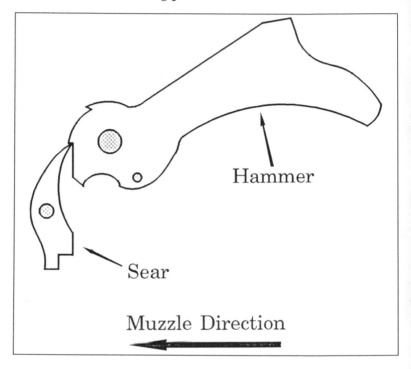

Colt-style hammer/sear.

As originally designed, Browning's 1911-type hammer/sear arrangement is "safe" with the hammer cocked *only* when the frame-mounted thumb safety is engaged. This externally actuated affirmative safety, among other things, internally engages the sear and hammer when the sear has engaged the hammer's full-cocked notch, and prevents the hammer from falling and striking the firing pin. Even if the sear were to slip or be jarred off the hammer's full-cock notch, the thumb safety should prevent it from falling and striking the firing pin. But if the thumb safety isn't fully engaged, the only thing keeping a cocked pistol from discharging is the rather tenuous hammer/sear engagement. Anyone who has carried 1911-type pistols, especially concealed, knows how easily these safeties can be "wiped" off. They also know the compulsion to continually verify full engagement of the safety.

Glock "Safe Action"

Glock pistols have no hammer. Likewise, they have no conventional sear, no mainspring, and no sear spring. Therefore, it is impossible for jarring or mechanical malfunction to cause the pistol to discharge unintentionally, as can happen with conventional pistols.

Glock pistols utilize an ingenious and marvelously simple design to fire ammunition. Instead of propelling the firing pin (5) forward by the force of a mainspring-loaded hammer strike, Glock firing pins are propelled by the force of a compressed firing-pin spring (7).

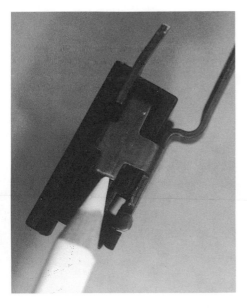

Here's how it works: Pulling the trigger also moves the trigger bar to the rear—remember, they're all part of a single assembly. The rearmost edge of the "cruciform sear plate" (an integral part of the trigger bar, it looks

The cruciform sear plate in place in the trigger mechanism housing, viewed from above. The plate is an integral part of the trigger bar, shown attached to the right side and extending out of the frame to the upper right.

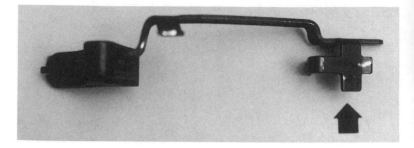

The complete trigger with trigger-bar assembly shown from above. If this were installed in a pistol, muzzle direction would be toward the left. The arrow indicates the cruciform sear plate.

A firing-pin assembly. Arrow #1 indicates the firing-pin tang, which hangs down and engages the rear portion of the cruciform sear plate. Arrow #2 indicates a pair of standard spring cups in place, retaining the firing-pin spring.

A firing pin shown in relative position above the trigger bar. If lowered slightly and installed in a receiver, the downward projecting firing-pin tang would engage the rear-projecting tab of the sear plate.

like a cross in the exploded diagram; hence the name) contacts the down-hanging projection (tang) at the rear of the firing pin, which then moves rearward with the trigger assembly, compressing the firing-pin spring. Eventually, the trigger bar travels rearward far enough so the tab at the back contacts the angled lip of the connector (24).

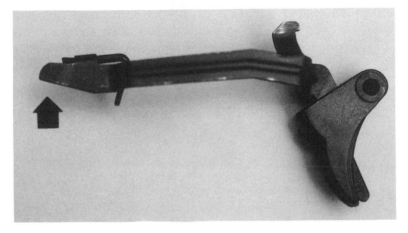

Trigger with trigger bar assembly shown from the left side (muzzle facing right). The arrow indicates the tab at the rearmost portion of the trigger bar. This is the tab that contacts the connector's angled ramp as the trigger is pulled. In this photo the trigger bar is coated with a black finish.

The receiver of a cutaway Model 19 showing the trigger bar tab in relation to the connector's angled ramp, with trigger in reset (full forward) position. In this photo the trigger bar is coated with a mottled gold-tone finish. The ejector can be seen on the far side of the receiver.

Here the trigger is in reset position, and the trigger-bar tab is as far forward of the connector's angled ramp as it ever is.

Here the trigger is shown pressed rearward until the "slack" has been taken up. The feeling of resistance at the end of the trigger's slack travel is caused by the tab contacting the angled ramp, as shown here.

This view shows the tab after sliding down the angled ramp when the trigger was pressed fully to the rear. The angle of the ramp determines how much trigger force is required; this is a standard five-pound angle.

More rearward movement causes the trigger bar (with integral sear plate still pushing the firing pin and compressing the firing-pin spring) to slide down the connector's angled lip. As trigger pull continues from this point, the back portion of the trigger bar (the sear plate) moves downward because the trigger-bar tab is sliding down the angled lip of the connector. At a certain point, the sear plate slips off the firing-pin tang that it was pushing against. By the time things have progressed this far, the firing-pin spring has been fully compressed, so when the sear plate drops down and slips beneath the firing-pin tang, the spring-loaded firing pin is powerfully propelled forward to strike the primer.

This is an ingenious design that eliminates several parts, significantly improving reliability and efficiency, as well as reducing weight. Like so many designs that are elegant in their simplicity, Glock's firing mechanism just makes sense.

Glock Safeties

Glock pistols incorporate three safeties, all of which: 1) are engaged when the pistol is in battery, 2) disengage automatically as the trigger is pulled, and 3) re-engage automatically when the slide moves forward into battery and the trigger is released.

All three safeties function automatically. Two of them are internal, and one is an external passive safety. Glock pistols have no affirmative safeties or decocking levers requiring conscious manipulation by the shooter. The three safeties are:

Trigger safety. Located on the trigger, it prevents the trigger from moving far enough to the rear to fire the pistol, unless the trigger safety is fully depressed. This is a passive safety that can be analogized to the grip safety on Colt's Government Model. It is disengaged by the shooter's finger on the trigger, but shooters generally won't even notice it during normal firing.

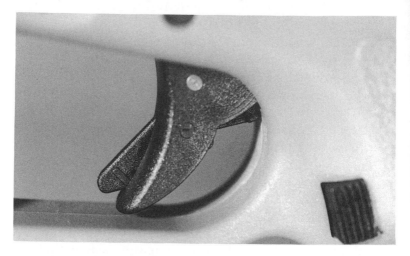

The trigger safety is the small projection on the trigger itself. In this view of the red training Model 17, the trigger pin can be seen just above the trigger, the left end of the slide lock just forward of the trigger pin, the magazine catch slightly behind and below the trigger, and the end of the slide stop lever above that.

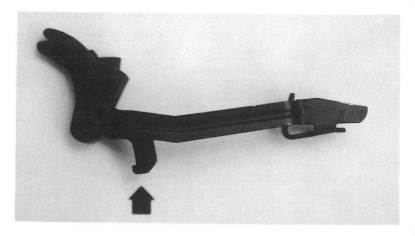

Trigger with trigger-bar assembly. The arrow indicates the upward-projecting arm that actuates the trigger safety.

The pencil indicates the trigger safety that is actuated by the upward-projecting trigger-bar arm (shown in the previous photo).

Firing-pin safety. Glock's firing-pin safety (#9, #10) is not a unique design. In fact, like virtually all others on modern pistols, it is substantially identical to the design introduced in 1983 by Colt for its Series 80 Government Models.

The firing pin on most pistols is positioned inside the rear portion of the slide, such that the pin's tip doesn't protrude at all. The firing pin is somewhat restrained in this position by the firing-pin spring. Absent a firing-pin safety, a pistol dropped on its muzzle could generate sufficient acceleration force that the spring-loaded firing pin might overcome its inertia and move forward, raising the possibility of a hard enough primer strike to cause detonation.

Firing-pin safeties are designed to prevent such an occurrence by mechanically blocking forward movement of the firing pin until the safety is released, which can be done only by pulling the trigger.

Glock's firing-pin safety consists of a pin (#9) with a tiny spring (#10) inside it. The safety projects into a cutout on the firing pin. Only pulling the trigger will disengage the firing-pin safety, allowing the firing pin to move far enough forward to discharge ammunition in the chamber.

Two views of the firing-pin safety on the cutaway Model 19. Here the trigger is in reset (full forward) position; the upward-projecting trigger-bar tab has not yet begun to actuate the firing-pin safety.

In this view the trigger has been pressed fully and the trigger bar arm has actuated the firing-pin safety, allowing the firing pin to move forward unrestrained.

A view of the firing-pin safety in position in the cutaway slide. The tiny spring inside the upper portion of the hourglass-shaped firing-pin safety can be seen here (the upper end of what is seen in the previous two photos).

Glock's firing-pin safety is about half an inch long, slightly less than a quarter inch at its largest diameter (the two end portions), and about an eighth of an inch in the middle.

Positioned vertically in the slide, between the extractor (#11) and the firing pin, it is spring-loaded to the safe position. This situates the upper larger-diameter portion (the longer of the two larger-diameter portions) into the firing-pin tunnel, adjacent to the firing-pin cutout. The large portions of the firing-pin safety are too big to permit the larger portion of the firing pin to get by. Unless and until the firing-pin safety is pushed up a bit, bringing its smaller portion into proximity of the firing pin, the firing pin is positively prevented from moving forward enough to protrude from the breechface and strike the primer of a chambered cartridge. The firing-pin safety is pushed up into firing position by a tab on the trigger bar that contacts it as the trigger is pulled.

Drop Safety. This internal safety prevents the firing pin from being released to strike a chambered primer unless and until the trigger is affirmatively pulled. With conventional sear/hammer arrangements, a jolt, such as from being dropped, can cause the sear to slip off the hammer notch, thus permitting the spring-loaded hammer to fall, strike the firing pin, and discharge a chambered round. With Glock's unique "safe action" design, and especially because of the drop safety, this cannot occur.

A view of the drop safety from the left side. In this photo the trigger mechanism housing has been lifted slightly up from its normal position in the receiver to allow viewing of the drop safety, which is normally hidden behind the left rear receiver rail, shown here. The drop safety is comprised of the left wing of the cruciform sear plate (the end of which can be seen in this photo), which fits inside the bi-level cutout in the left side of the trigger mechanism housing. Here the trigger is in the full forward position.

The drop safety works like this: as the sear plate is moved to the rear, pushing the firing-pin tang back and spring-loading the firing pin, it is prevented from premature release (which would result in instantaneous firing) by the drop safety. To prevent premature firing-pin release (the equivalent of a conventional sear slipping off a hammer notch), the sear plate is physically constrained from dropping below the firing-pin tang (the only way it can be released to move forward) by the drop safety.

As with so many of Gaston Glock's designs, the drop safety is marvelously simple: the left wing of the cruciform sear plate protrudes through a bi-level slot (higher at the front, lower at the rear) in the trigger mechanism housing (23). This prevents the sear plate from dropping (whether

from a jolt or for any other reason) too early and prematurely releasing the firing pin. Only when the trigger has been
pulled virtually all the way back can the left wing of the
sear plate drop into the lower portion of the slot, allowing
the entire rear portion of the trigger bar (of which the sear
plate is a part) to drop and release the firing pin.

Function-Testing Glock Safeties

To function-test Glock safeties, it is first necessary to
fieldstrip the pistol. Detailed instructions for this are provided in Chapter 12.

Trigger Safety
Remove the slide from the receiver. The trigger will be
to the rear. CAVEAT: Never pull the trigger when the slide
is removed (except using the following method) or
locked back.

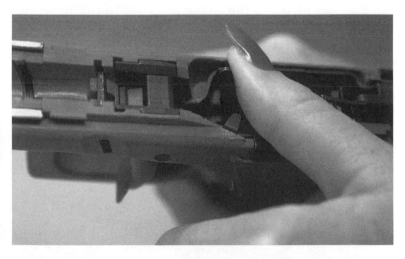

*Never move the trigger mechanism with the slide removed without maintaining coun-
teropposing (forward and rearward) pressure. This is accomplished by pressing rearward
on the trigger with the trigger finger and simultaneously pressing forward on the upward-
projecting trigger bar tab with the thumb of the nonshooting hand. It is necessary to use
this procedure when function-testing the trigger safety.*

To reset the trigger, hold the receiver in a normal shooting position, finger gently on the trigger. Using the thumb of your nonshooting hand, push the trigger bar's vertical extension forward; you should be able to hear (and feel) the trigger safety reset. The trigger should remain in the forward position.

Next, with the thumb of your nonshooting hand, exert and maintain a little forward pressure on the trigger bar's vertical extension. While maintaining forward pressure on the trigger bar, gently press the trigger until it returns all the way to the rear.

If the trigger remained forward when you pushed it there, then returned to the full rearward position when you pulled it, proper engagement and release of the trigger safety is verified.

Firing-Pin Safety

Remove the barrel from the slide. Hold the slide muzzle down. The tip of the firing pin should not protrude from the firing-pin hole in the breechface.

This is what a retracted firing pin looks like when performing a firing-pin safety function test. The firing pin's nose can be seen inside its channel. Note the outline of previously fired ammunition cartridges on the breechface.

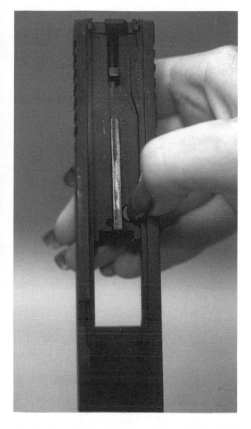

Still holding the slide muzzle down, depress the firing-pin safety with your fingertip. The firing pin should fall forward, the tip protruding out of the firing-pin hole in the breechface.

Next, release the firing-pin safety, then reset the firing pin by pushing the firing-pin tang toward the rear. The firing pin's tip should retract so it no longer protrudes from the firing-pin hole in the breechface. It should remain inside when the firing-pin tang is pushed forward without the firing-pin safety being depressed.

To function test the firing-pin safety, hold the field-stripped slide muzzle end down while depressing the firing-pin safety, as demonstrated here.

There is another method of checking the firing-pin safety that doesn't require removal of the barrel. First, shake the slide longitudinally (fore and aft); you should hear very little or no rattling. Next, depress and hold the firing-pin safety and shake the slide fore and aft. You should now be able to hear the firing pin rattling loud and clear.

Depress the firing-pin safety and push the firing-pin tang forward; it should stay there. Using a light, look carefully to see the firing pin's tip protruding from the breechface. Return the tang to the rear position, then push forward without depressing the firing-pin safety. The firing pin should not move, and its tip should not protrude from the breechface.

Drop Safety

There is no practical way to function-test the drop safety.

Glock Pistols' Operating Sequence

In Battery, Trigger Forward

When the pistol is fully assembled and in ready-to-fire configuration, all three safeties are engaged. Further, in this condition:

1. *There is a small (3/32-inch) space between the trigger safety and the frame.* If you look at a side view of the pistol this space can easily be seen. It is the gap behind the rear of the trigger safety and in front of the frame.

This gap is maintained by the firing-pin spring, which is applying forward pressure on the firing pin, which in turn is applying forward pressure on the trigger. Remember, the sear plate is an integral part of the trigger bar, which is attached to the trigger (the whole thing is an assembly). So when the spring-loaded firing pin's tang pushes forward against the rearmost end of the sear plate, it holds the trigger fully forward; thus, the gap is maintained.

2. *The end of the trigger bar is about 1/8 inch forward of the connector's angled lip.* In this position, the sear plate (indeed, the entire rear portion of the trigger bar) cannot drop beneath the firing-pin tang, thus preventing release of the firing pin and its subsequent forward movement to strike a chambered primer.

Although the end of the trigger bar is about 1/8 inch forward of the connector's angled lip, the trigger itself must be pressed back about 5/16 inch before this contact is made. That 5/16-inch "free play" is often referred to as slack, or trigger slack.

3. *The bi-level slot in the left side of the trigger mechanism housing*, into which the left wing of the cruciform-shaped sear plate extends (this combination comprises the drop safety), *prevents the sear plate from dropping below the firing-pin tang*, which is applying forward pressure against the rear of the sear plate. If the sear plate were allowed to drop below the firing-pin tang, the firing pin could move forward and discharge a chambered round of ammunition.

4. *The vertically extending tab on the trigger bar*, located inside the right side of the receiver and projecting upward into the underside of the slide, *is immediately forward of the firing-pin safety.*

5. *The firing pin is held slightly retracted from the breechface*; it isn't allowed to protrude, so it cannot contact a primer in the chamber.

First Part of Trigger Travel

When the trigger is pressed and begins to move:

6. *The trigger safety is disengaged.* As the trigger safety is pressed flush with the face of the trigger, the rear end of the safety retracts into, and flush with, the upper rear portion of the trigger. This allows the trigger safety to clear the receiver as the trigger is moved to the rear.

7. *The vertically extending tab on the trigger bar presses the firing-pin safety upward*, disengaging it.

8. *The trigger bar moves the firing pin to the rear* (accomplished by the sear plate exerting rearward force on the firing-pin tang) as the trigger is pulled further back; this rearward movement partially compresses the firing-pin spring.

When the tab of the trigger bar contacts the connector's angled lip, the pistol is said to be cocked. Unlike conventional pistols that will remain cocked without trigger pressure, Glocks will "uncock" automatically if, at this point, trigger pressure is removed. At this point, the firing-pin spring (1 1/2 to 1 9/16 inches long when relaxed, and 1 1/4 to 1 5/16 inches long when installed with no trigger pressure applied) has been compressed roughly an additional 1/8 inch.

As the Trigger Moves Further to the Rear

9. *The trigger bar*, having contacted the connector's angled lip, *is forced to move downward* (following the angle of the connector's lip) as trigger pressure moves it further to the rear.

This downward movement of the trigger bar causes the sear plate, the integral rear portion of the trigger bar, to move downward as well.

10. *The firing pin is released and driven forward* by the compressed firing-pin spring (when the trigger has been pulled enough to move the trigger bar back far enough to slide down the connector's angled lip sufficiently to drop the sear plate below the downward extension of the firing-pin tang).

Once released, the firing pin travels forward through the tunnel in the rear portion of the slide. The firing pin's tip protrudes through the opening in the breechface and strikes the chambered primer, discharging the round.

As Detonation Occurs

11. *Recoil begins moving the slide (with the locked-up barrel) to the rear, and the extractor (part of the slide assembly) begins removing (extracting) the empty case from the chamber.*

12. *The barrel is unlocked from the slide* when the slide assembly has moved to the rear about 1/16 inch. The rear, or breech, end of the barrel drops down and nestles into the locking block, providing sufficient clearance for the slide to pass over on its way to full rearward extension.

13. *A milled ramp* (actually a wide spot on the upper

right-side slide rail) *pushes the connector inward* about 3/32 inch when the slide has moved to the rear about 1/2 inch. This allows the trigger spring's relatively slight forward pressure to "pop" the sear plate back up to the level it was before being forced down by the connector's angled lip.

14. *The extracted cartridge is ejected* (i.e., thrown out the ejection port on the pistol's right side). This happens when the extracted cartridge and the slide move together to the rear, finally causing the cartridge's base to strike the ejector.

The ejector is part of the trigger-mechanism housing (23). It projects forward from the housing on the left side and is about 1/2 inch behind the slide-stop lever (27).

15. *The slide reaches the end of its rearward travel and reverses direction.* As the slide travels to the rear, recoil energy diminishes while, simultaneously, the recoil spring is being compressed, storing its energy in preparation for driving the slide forward.

When the slide reaches its rearmost position, recoil energy is gone and the compressed recoil spring is allowed to take over. It begins moving the slide forward.

Glock slides and recoil springs are balanced against recoil better than virtually any other pistol, which contributes to low felt recoil and comfortable shooting.

16. *The trigger moves forward; it and the trigger safety are reset.* As the slide begins its forward travel, the firing-pin tang catches on the rear edge of the sear plate and pushes the trigger bar forward. If trigger pressure has been released, or is subsequently released, the trigger safety will re-engage, and the trigger will reset as the slide moves forward into battery.

17. *A fresh cartridge is chambered.* About the same time as the events in item 16 are occurring, the bottom portion of the breechface catches the upper edge of the top ammunition cartridge in the magazine. As the slide continues forward, that ammunition cartridge is pushed forward as

well, stripping it off the magazine and eventually pushing it up the feed ramp and into the firing chamber.

If the magazine is empty, a ridge on the magazine follower pushes the slide-stop lever up, causing it to engage the notch cut into the left side of the slide. This stops the slide's forward movement at that point, holding it open.

18. *Lock-up occurs.* As the slide, in its final forward-movement stages, goes into full battery, the breech end of the barrel is moved upward and locked into position, held there by forward pressure on the upper rear face of the chamber by the breechface and rearward pressure on the front barrel lug by the slide lock.

19. *The firing pin is once again retracted inside its tunnel*, slightly behind the breechface, once the pistol is in battery.

20. *Finally, all three safeties are re-engaged*, and the pistol is ready to be fired.

CHAPTER 12

Glock Maintenance

istol maintenance usually is thought of as falling into one of three categories: 1) routine maintenance and cleaning, 2) minor repair and modification, and 3) in-depth repair and customizing. The second category is sometimes explored by those possessing both an adventurous nature and, hopefully, greater smithing skills than the average amateur tinkerer. Category three should be considered the exclusive province of qualified pistolsmiths.

The above applies to virtually every pistol ever built—except the Glock. Because Glocks have no hand-fitted parts (every part fits out-of-the-box), there is no smithing required. All that's necessary to do anything and everything to Glock pistols are the knowledge and skills taught in Glock Armorer Training.

If you read and understand the contents of this chapter, you will be exposed to all the information in the factory Glock Armorer Training course. You will not, of course, have the benefit of learning to disassemble, examine, and reassemble your Glock pistol under the supervision of an instructor, but if you carefully follow the guidelines in this chapter, you will be able to do it.

Once you have learned what's here, you'll be

able to service and maintain your Glock pistol completely independently. The only thing you'll need is a source from which to obtain Glock parts, as Glock sells parts only to certified Glock armorers.

Routine Glock Maintenance

Routine pistol maintenance can range from doing nothing at all to fastidious disassembly after each and every firing, and everything in between. Whatever degree of maintenance you choose, however, it's easier to accomplish on a Glock pistol than on any other.

How often and to what extent pistols should be cleaned are controversial topics, about which there's a wide range of disagreement. We'll discuss what's appropriate for Glock pistols in a bit, but first let's go over some general cleaning and maintenance basics.

No pistol cleaning should be attempted by merely locking the slide open and running a cleaning rod through the barrel from the muzzle end. Such a technique falls into the "revolver mentality" category (in most cases, it's the only way to clean revolver barrels), but it can cause problems for pistols. One of those problems is excessive solvent build-up in the receiver and slide. This facilitates the accumulation of other substances and can lead to malfunctions. Using proper solvents and lubricants helps, but it's best to avoid muzzle-entry bore cleaning, regardless of what's used.

Never attempt to clean a semiautomatic handgun without first fieldstripping it. Many newer pistols, notably the "wondernines" (high-capacity 9mm Parabellum semiautomatic handguns designed after the mid-1970s), can be fieldstripped without any tools, something that was difficult or impossible with pistols of earlier design. Of all the new high-technology pistols, Glock is considered by many to have the easiest "takedown" method.

Fieldstripping

Slide Removal

To fieldstrip a Glock pistol, it must first be unloaded:

1. Point the muzzle in a safe direction.
2. Remove the magazine.
3. Lock the slide open.
4. Verify that the chamber is empty.

Thorough verification of an empty chamber requires both a visual and a tactile check to ensure no ammunition is present. First look as far into the chamber as possible, then feel with your little finger to ascertain absolutely that there is no chambered cartridge.

Once the pistol is verified to be unloaded:

1. Point the muzzle in a safe direction.
2. Close the action.
3. Press the trigger until it's fully to the rear.

Now the pistol is in battery, fully decocked, and ready for slide removal.

From this point, to remove the slide:

1. Hold the pistol so that the slide can be pulled back about 1/10 inch. This can be done by grasping the gun as Glock suggests, wrapping your thumb around the recurve area of the backstrap, and wrapping your fingers over the top of the slide, your forefinger just ahead of the rear sight. Or, alternatively, you can grasp the rear of the slide with your first two or three fingers wrapped over the top, ahead of and over the rear sight, and your thumb around the recurve area of the backstrap.

The Glock-recommended grip is used to retract the slide about 1/8 inch while the slide lock is held down.

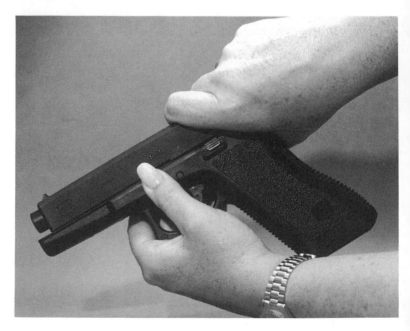

An alternate method of grasping the gun to accomplish slide release for fieldstripping.

The red training Model 17 shown with slide detached for fieldstripping.

The fieldstripped components of the slide.

Regardless of which grasp is used, when the slide is pulled back about 1/10 inch, hold it there and:

2. Using the thumb and forefinger of your other hand, simultaneously pull down and hold both sides of the slide lock.
3. Release your grasp on the slide; it will move to, or just a bit forward of, the "in battery" position.
4. Release your hold on the slide stop ends.
5. Move the slide forward until it comes completely off the receiver.

Barrel Removal

With the slide lying upside down on a table or other suitable surface:

1. Release the recoil spring by pushing slightly forward on the large end of the recoil-spring tube (it rests in the first, or lower, step on the forward side of the front barrel lug), lifting it.

A fieldstripped Model 17.

CAUTION: The recoil spring is under tension. Use care to control it and the recoil-spring tube whenever working with them. Wear eye protection.

2. Remove the recoil spring and recoil-spring tube.
3. Grasp the barrel at the chamber (by the lugs), lift it slightly, and slide it forward a bit.
4. Remove the barrel from the slide.

The pistol is now fieldstripped. Further disassembly, except for the magazine, is unnecessary for routine cleaning and maintenance, and should not be attempted without suitable training.

Magazine Disassembly
Any and all magazines used for defense should be disassembled and cleaned whenever your pistol is cleaned. To disassemble a Glock magazine:

1. Hold the magazine upside down.
2. Grasp the magazine tube with your thumb and forefinger very close to the floorplate, where the small tabs are (center of magazine tube sides).
3. Press inward far enough for the tabs to clear their corresponding notches in the floorplate.
4. While holding the tabs in, slide the floorplate forward until the notches have cleared the tabs.

Magazine disassembly tabs.

A partially removed magazine floorplate, revealing the magazine spring.

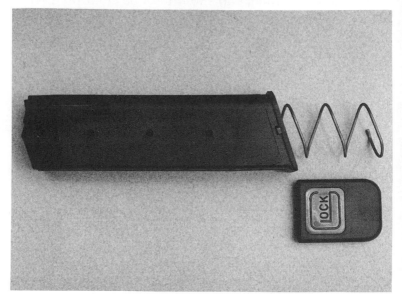

The floorplate has been removed, allowing the magazine spring to extend fully. If the spring in this position extends out of the magazine tube farther than the length of the floorplate (shown here) or less than the floorplate width, it should be replaced.

CAUTION: The magazine spring is under tension. Maintain downward pressure on it with your thumb while disassembling the magazine. Wear eye protection.

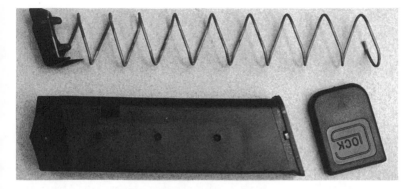

The four components of a Glock pistol magazine. Here the follower is still attached to the spring.

5. Controlling the magazine spring until it is no longer under tension, slide the floorplate all the way off.
6. Remove the magazine spring and follower.

Cleaning the Fieldstripped Glock

The Glock factory suggests periodic cleaning to ensure proper functioning. While it cannot be disputed that cleaning at reasonable intervals is appropriate, considerable controversy exists about how often a pistol should be cleaned.

When revolvers were state-of-the-art for defense handguns, conventional wisdom held that guns should be cleaned after every firing, or very nearly so. Similar, although somewhat moderated, thinking continued into the age of high-tech pistols, despite developments that have made such practice unnecessary.

Many modern pistols require far less frequent cleaning, with the exception of certain customized semiautomatics that have been "accurized" for competition purposes. It is also the case that many cleaning, lubricating, and preservation products are more durable than their predecessors, requiring far less frequent replenishment through weapon cleaning. This is especially true for some combination cleaning/lubricating/preserving products.

By design, Glock pistols require somewhat less frequent cleaning, and significantly less lubrication and preservatives, than do conventional pistols.

Cleaning, Lubricating, and Preserving Solutions

For many years there were only petroleum-based solvents, lubricants, and preservatives. Petroleum-based solutions may protect metal parts from rusting, pitting, and other forms of deterioration, but they are problematic, if not downright dangerous, on guns used for defense. This is especially true for guns that are carried on the person. Petroleum-based solutions attract, and combine with, dust, dirt, and airborne contaminates to form a sludgelike compound that severely inhibits proper pistol function.

Combination cleaners/lubricants/preservatives, especially Teflon-or silicon-based substances, are better than petroleum-based ones, but they only reduce the problem—not eliminate it. Additionally, some of these products have vigorous penetrating qualities (especially silicon-based solutions) that can be disastrous for defense guns.

Virtually all traditional gun cleaning, lubricating, and preserving products do, to some degree, facilitate sludge formation. It is, therefore, necessary when using them to clean guns fairly frequently, even if they haven't been fired, just to ensure that they'll operate properly when needed. Moreover, unburned powder and other residual products of the firing process greatly exacerbate the problem. Gun oils and other similar products require that guns to which they've been applied be cleaned, and they must be replenished frequently.

"Gun oil" is so profoundly linked with firearms that, for many, a gun literally dripping with it is normal or even desirable. Fear of oxidization, combined with a lack of understanding of the problems associated with excess oiling, has bred generations of gun owners who don't realize how counterproductive it is to coat their defense guns with the smelly, greasy substances bestowed by tradition.

Prolix

There is a substance, specifically for firearms, designed to avoid the problems associated with petroleum-based products (traditional "gun oils") that really shouldn't be used on most firearms. That substance is called Prolix.

Prolix contains no petroleum, Teflon, graphite, silicone, or greases. It doesn't attract dirt, dust, or other airborne contaminants. Prolix cleans, lubricates, and preserves firearms.

A 1-ounce bottle of Prolix.

Conceived and developed by Phillip J. Levy and associates, Prolix is a truly amazing product for total gun care. Phil Levy was an industrial technician at a pattern-making foundry. While recuperating from an injury, he came up with the idea that eventually became Prolix. Developed entirely in the laboratory exclusively for gun care, Prolix uses the base solvent 111 Trichlorethane combined with some lubricants developed for the space industry, plus various secret additives.

Prolix cleans gun parts amazingly easily and thoroughly, then leaves an optimum amount of lubricant and a "dry-to-the-touch" protective film. It will not "flash off," as will virtually all other products. It is virtually nontoxic, nonflammable, and will not freeze down to -80°F.

Cleaning New Glock Pistols

New Glock pistols should be cleaned prior to firing. All heavy preservative oil (not the copper-colored lubricant to be discussed in a moment) put on by the factory should be wiped away. Be certain to carefully remove all such oil from the bore using a clean, dry cleaning patch or swab.

Before shipping, the Glock factory adds a copper-colored combination lubricant and preservative to various internal parts. This substance can be found on the slide rails, the connector, and the firing-pin safety, among other places. It should not be removed during the initial prefiring cleaning, as it helps during the break-in period and aids in long-term lubrication of the slide. Remnants of this substance are likely to remain for quite some time, but that's okay. Just leave it there.

In addition to removal of the heavy oil applied to the pistol prior to shipping, routine cleaning procedures should be followed before firing a new Glock for the first time.

Routine Cleaning

The traditional method of cleaning a pistol barrel is to run a solvent-soaked patch, swab, or brush through the bore (from the breech, or chamber, end), then set the barrel aside for a while so the solvent can soak into the bore. This can be done using Prolix (or, if you must, some other gun solvent) on a clean patch or on the nylon brush supplied with every Glock pistol.

The best method, however, is to immerse the barrel in a small dish containing Prolix. Immerse the recoil spring, recoil spring tube, and slide in Prolix also.

CAUTION: Read the section on night sights in Chapter 10 before immersing Armson or Meprolite night sights in Prolix or any other solvent.

After a few minutes, wipe off the recoil spring and the recoil-spring tube. Do not attempt to rub all the Prolix off; merely wipe the surfaces dry. As an alternative, use compressed air or a hair dryer to blow-dry the parts.

Next, wipe or blow off the slide. Using a clean, dry toothbrush, pipe cleaner, or swab, thoroughly clean the breechface and extractor hook; also wipe the slide rail grooves and exposed underside areas of the slide. If necessary, to remove stubborn debris apply a small amount of Prolix before lightly scrubbing stubborn areas.

CAUTION: Thoroughly dry the breechface, firing-pin tunnel, and associated areas. Residual fluids in these areas can invade and contaminate primers, rendering them inoperative, especially in pistols carried or stored muzzle-down.

By this time the barrel has soaked sufficiently. If you're using the immersion method, soak the receiver in Prolix when you remove the barrel. Wipe off the outside of the barrel, feed ramp, and chamber, then run a soft brush (like the one Glock supplies with each pistol) completely through the bore. Never reverse direction in the bore; push the brush completely through, then pull it back out. It is not necessary to scrub the bore. Run a clean, dry patch or swab through the bore once or twice to finish the job.

Dry the receiver the way the other parts were dried. Using a clean, dry toothbrush, pipe cleaner, or swab, clean the rails, ejector, trigger bar, top of sear plate, and other areas where powder residue can be seen or is known to accumulate, such as inside the magazine well.

NOTE: Now is a good time to function-test the firing-pin safety and the trigger safety. Follow the procedures described in the "Function-Testing Glock Safeties" section of Chapter 11.

Lubricating Glock Pistols

Truth be known, Glock pistols require little or no lubrication. The *Glock Armorer's Manual*, published in June 1989 by Glock, Inc., and other Glock-generated materials supplied in connection with Glock Armorer's certification training, suggest only three drops of oil be used to lubricate the entire pistol. Here is what Glock says:

1. Using a finger, apply one drop of lubricant to the outside of the barrel, especially on the hood, lugs, and wherever rub marks appear.
2. Without adding more lubricant, use the same finger to apply some lubricant to the underside of the slide where the barrel has rubbed.
3. Apply a second drop of lubricant to a finger and wipe it across the receiver rails.
4. Apply one final drop of oil to the trigger bar, where the trigger bar and connector meet at the angle of the connector.

An excellent publication entitled *Glock Armorer Training Program*, prepared by Cathy Lane (Cathy and Jerry Lane and their company, Offshoots Training Institute, do contract training of law enforcement personnel for Glock, Inc.), states, following the above lubrication recommendations, "No other oil is necessary since there is no metal-to-metal abrasion of parts which causes wear." In its *Armorer's Manual*, Glock cautions: "Do not overlubricate your GLOCK pistol, as large quantities of oil or grease will collect unburnt powder and other residue, which could interfere with proper functioning of your GLOCK pistol." If you use Prolix to clean and lubricate your Glock pistol, it is not necessary even to apply those three drops, as described above. The residual left by Prolix after cleaning and drying is sufficient to lubricate the pistol.

Complete Disassembly/Reassembly of Glock Pistols

Only three tools are required to completely disassemble Glock pistols:
1. 3/32-inch (2.5mm) pin punch, craftsman #42882WF

2. 1/8-inch (3mm) blade screwdriver, craftsman #41589WF
3. Long- or needle-nose pliers, any common type

Realistically, only the 3/32-inch pin punch (called "the Glock Armorer's tool" by many) is used for most of the work you'll ever do on a Glock pistol. But it's a good idea to have the other two items, as suggested by Glock in its *Armorer's Manual*. The *Glock Armorer Training Program* materials suggest a thorough armorer's kit should also contain an X-ACTO-type knife with an assortment of blades and a padded vise. To those things I would add that some may wish to consider a Glock sight installation device. There is also a special tool required to install the front sight on Armson and Meprolight night sights (a different tool for each).

Slide Disassembly
The following description assumes a fieldstripped slide (recoil spring, recoil-spring tube, and barrel removed). To completely disassemble the slide:

1. Hold the slide muzzle-down on a table or other suitable flat surface, fingers of support hand wrapped around the slide, thumb on the slide cover plate (15).
2. Insert the tip of your punch (held in your strong hand) into the space between the firing-pin tang and the spacer sleeve (6). Push the spring-loaded spacer sleeve down (toward the muzzle end of the slide) to relieve pressure on the slide cover plate.
3. Gently, slide the slide cover plate partway off, just enough to release the extractor depressor plunger assembly (extractor depressor plunger [12], extractor depressor plunger spring [13], and spring-loaded bearing [14]).
4. Remove the punch.
5. Carefully remove the slide cover plate the rest of

the way, keeping your support hand thumb over the end of the slide to prevent spring-launching any components under the slide cover plate.

CAUTION: The firing-pin assembly (firing pin, spacer sleeve, firing-pin spring, and spring cups [8]) and extractor depressor plunger assembly are under tension. Use care to prevent ejection during removal. Wear eye protection.

To use the slide as a jig to hold the firing pin for disassembly, remove the firing pin from its channel, invert it, and insert the short end back in the channel, as shown here. The tang must be offset (shown here to the left) so the pin assembly won't go all the way down into the channel. Note the spring-loaded bearing and the end of the extractor depressor plunger spring (just to the right of the firing pin) protruding from their place in the slide.

6. Remove the firing-pin assembly.
7. Remove the extractor depressor plunger assembly.

8. Depress firing-pin safety and remove extractor (use finger, punch, or tap gently on table if extractor fails to drop out).
9. Remove firing-pin safety and firing-pin-safety spring.

The slide is now completely disassembled, except for the firing-pin assembly.

Disassembly of Firing-Pin Assembly

To facilitate disassembly (and reassembly) of the spring-loaded firing-pin assembly, use the slide as a jig:

1. Place the slide muzzle-down on a table or other suitable flat surface.
2. Insert the firing-pin assembly upside down, or backwards (plastic spacer sleeve down), into the firing-pin tunnel. Keep the firing-pin tang to one side so it doesn't slide down into its normal channel.
3. Pull the firing-pin spring down and hold it there.
4. Remove the spring cups and slowly release the firing-pin spring (just allow it to relax).

CAUTION: The firing-pin spring must be clean and dry and held firmly to avoid uncontrolled launching of the spring cups. Wear eye protection.

5. Remove the firing pin and the spacer sleeve from the slide and separate them.

The firing-pin assembly is now completely disassembled.

Reassembly of Firing-Pin Assembly

Reassemble the firing-pin assembly by reversing the disassembly procedures:

1. Insert the tip (the part that hits the primer) of the

firing pin into the end spacer sleeve with the open channel. The firing-pin lug should go all the way into the spacer sleeve channel so nearly all of the firing pin sticks out of the sleeve.

2. Insert the spacer sleeve with firing pin into the firing-pin tunnel of the slide, keeping the firing-pin tang off to one side.
3. Place the firing-pin spring over the firing pin. The spring should stick up about 3/4 inch past the firing pin's tip.
4. Firmly grasp the firing-pin spring and pull it at least 1/4 inch below the shoulder, where the narrow portion of the firing pin begins; hold it there.

CAUTION: The firing-pin spring must be clean and dry and held firmly to avoid uncontrolled launching. Wear eye protection.

5. One at a time, while holding the firing-pin spring down as described in item #4, carefully replace the spring cups, then gently relax the firing-pin spring to retain them in place.
6. Remove the firing-pin assembly from the slide.

The firing-pin assembly is now reassembled.

Slide Reassembly
It is important to reassemble the slide components in the following sequence:

1. Lay the slide on its left side on a table or other suitable flat surface, ejection port facing up.
2. Replace the extractor.
3. Holding the extractor in place, turn the slide so it is resting upside down (on the sights).
4. Still holding the extractor gently with your thumb, insert the firing-pin safety with your other hand.

Glock Maintenance

NOTE: As the firing-pin safety is inserted, the extractor—which was flush against the side of the slide—will jut out slightly, then return to flush again as the firing-pin safety goes fully into position. It is important that this "flush-out-flush" sequence occurs during firing-pin safety replacement.

5. Replace the extractor depressor plunger assembly, the longer solid end first, spring-loaded bearing last. Once the extractor depressor plunger assembly is in place, the extractor and firing-pin safety will remain in place without being held.
6. Replace the firing-pin assembly, inserting the small end of the firing pin down into the firing-pin tunnel, and the firing-pin tang as far as it will go down into the channel. Only about 1/8 inch of the spacer sleeve should be sticking out of the firing-pin tunnel.
7. Holding the spacer sleeve down against the pressure of the firing-pin spring (using the large end of the punch helps), slide the slide cover plate partway into position, at least sufficiently to hold down the spacer sleeve.
8. Holding the spring-loaded bearing down with the tip of the punch, slide the slide cover plate all the way into position until it snaps in place.
9. Replace the barrel.
10. Fit the open end of the recoil spring into the recess behind the muzzle end of the slide.
11. Carefully compress the recoil spring, allowing the small end of the recoil-spring tube to extend through the hole in the muzzle end of the slide.

CAUTION: The recoil spring, once compressed, will be under tension. Use care to control it and the recoil-spring tube whenever working with them. Wear eye protection.

12. Seat the large end of the recoil-spring tube into the semicircular recess (lower step) on the front face of the forward barrel lug.

The slide is now reassembled.

The chamber end of a Glock barrel showing the barrel lugs. Note the semicircular lower step that mates with the large end of the recoil spring tube.

A recoil spring tube in place in the semicircular lower step of the front barrel lug.

Receiver Disassembly

Glock Models 17, 17L, and 19 have two pins; Models 20, 21, 22, and 23 have three. The third pin is above and slightly behind the trigger pin; it should always be removed and replaced before the locking block's lower pin.

NOTE: All Glock pins should be removed from left to right and replaced from right to left.

Disassemble the receiver as follows:

1. Pushing from left to right, remove the upper (third) pin from the locking block (not applicable to Models 17, 17L, and 19).
2. Holding the receiver right side down against a table or other suitable flat surface, grasp the slide-stop lever with the thumb and forefinger of your support hand.

A locking block from a Model 17. Note there is only one hole because 9mm Glocks have only a single locking block pin.

An inverted locking block with pin.

A slide-stop lever.

3. With the punch in your strong hand, push out the trigger pin (pushing from left to right). Both shifting the slide-stop lever fore and aft and holding the receiver slightly off the table facilitate trigger pin removal. Shifting the slide-stop lever fore and aft relieves tension on the trigger pin from the slide-stop lever's spring. Holding the receiver slightly off the table eliminates the possibility that you'll be trying to push the trigger pin out when it's pressing against the table.
4. Remove the slide-stop lever by gently pulling it back, slightly up, and out.
5. Insert the punch beneath the lateral bar of the locking block, entering from the rear, the punch lying diagonally across the left side of the frame in the area where the slide-stop lever is usually located. Using the punch as a lever across the left receiver rail, gently pry up the locking block until it can be removed by hand, and remove it.
6. Pushing from left to right, use the punch to remove the trigger mechanism housing pin.
7. Insert the punch under the ejector, entering from the left side, punch roughly at right angles to the ejector. Using the punch as a lever across the left receiver rail, gently pry up the ejector until the trigger-mechanism housing assembly can be removed by hand, and remove it.
8. Lay the receiver on its side. Using the punch, depress the slide-lock spring and hold it, allowing the slide lock to fall out of the receiver. (You may have to hold the receiver slightly off the table to get the slide lock to fall out.)
9. Remove the slide-lock spring. (You may have to invert the receiver and tap it gently on the table or even pry it up to get the slide-lock spring to fall out.)

Disassembly of Trigger-Mechanism Housing Assembly

Hold the trigger-mechanism housing in your support hand; hold the trigger in your strong hand. Then:

1. Pull slightly forward on the trigger and move it away from you just a bit to release the left wing of the cruciform-shaped sear plate from the drop-safety slot. This will allow the trigger bar and trigger to hang free from the trigger-mechanism housing, connected only by the trigger spring, unless the pistol has a New York trigger spring installed. If a New York trigger spring is installed, the above release and separation of the sear plate from the trigger-mechanism housing will be easy, obvious, and will sometimes occur on its own.
2. Disconnect the trigger spring from both the trigger-mechanism housing and the trigger bar (unnecessary if a New York trigger spring is installed).
3. Remove the connector from the trigger-mechanism housing (you may have to pry it up to get it loose).

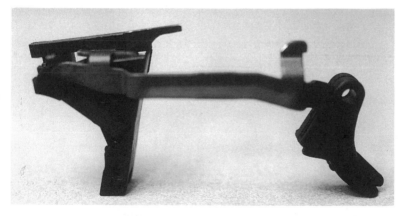

A trigger with trigger bar assembly mated with a trigger mechanism housing. This particular unit has a New York trigger installed, which is why the rear of the sear plate is pushed up slightly. A coil-type spring would apply downward pressure.

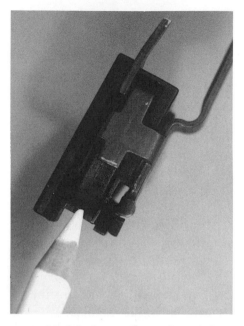

A view of the mated assemblies from above. The pencil is pointing to the New York trigger spring.

Magazine Catch Removal

This is the only task that requires the 1/8-inch blade screwdriver (a small knife blade will also suffice) and a pair of long- or needle-nose pliers. Remove the magazine catch as follows:

1. Hold the right side of the magazine catch on the outside of the grip so that the catch doesn't move.
2. Insert the screwdriver or knife blade down the magazine well from the top. Place the blade on the left side of the magazine-catch spring.
3. Push the magazine-catch spring to the right, toward the notch. Move it out through the notch to the top of the magazine catch.
4. Remove the magazine catch from the right side of the receiver.
5. Using the long- or needle-nose pliers, remove the magazine-catch spring through the top of the magazine well.

The receiver is completely disassembled.

Receiver Reassembly

Receiver reassembly is accomplished by assembling the components in reverse order from the way they were disassembled. There are, however, a few things to be noted:

1. On Models 17 and 22, the short end of the slide-lock spring goes into the receiver vertically, the long end horizontally.
2. The slide lock goes into position with the milled lateral channel facing to the rear of the receiver. (If the slide lock is installed backward, the lip on the front of the barrel lug will have nothing to positively secure it.) Once installed, check the slide lock for proper installation by pulling it down; it should snap up.
3. There is no right or wrong direction for the original (coil-type) trigger spring, but it must be installed between the trigger-mechanism housing and the trigger bar in an "S" configuration (with the gaps on the end hooks facing in opposite directions). You can check for proper installation when the pistol is fully reassembled by allowing the slide to slam into battery, from fully open, under full force of the recoil spring. If the trigger spring is reversed (twisted), the trigger won't return (reset) as it should.
4. When reinstalling the slide-stop lever, check to see that it is spring-loaded to the down position (it should snap down when lifted and released), and that you can see the end of the spring under the locking block.

That's it. That's all there is to completely disassembling a Glock pistol and fully reassembling it again. With a little practice, you'll find yourself doing it amazingly fast. It's truly unremarkable to replace a broken trigger spring in about one minute.

CHAPTER 13

Design Features

ny examination of a particular handgun's operational and tactical advantages should rest on a foundation of the
fundamental notion that the semiautomatic (pistol) is tactically superior to
the revolver. When the advantages
being examined are those of Glocks, it is
especially important that said tactical
superiority be clearly understood.

Revolvers vs. Pistols

Some consider suggestions that pistols are better than revolvers for defense
to be fightin' words. But, in fact, no well-
informed, objective person can think otherwise.
Emotions and tradition aside, revolvers are not
state-of-the-art personal defense guns.

Indeed, Americans are global Johnny-come-
latelies in that regard. Virtually everywhere else
in the world, pistols have been acknowledged as
tactically superior to revolvers for decades. But
not in America, where revolvers have enthralled
most of the populace throughout the country's
history. The major exception in this century was
the military, which, as many know, adopted the
venerable Colt Government Model in 1911.

Grips

Of the numerous tactical advantages semiautos have over revolvers, one of the most noticeable is the pistol's much more natural grip angle. This is especially true for modern semiautos. If you're one of those folks who believe it's just the opposite, take someone who has never fired a revolver—someone who was introduced to shooting on pistols and has never shot anything else—and put a revolver in his or her hand. Watch what happens: the person will look at it aghast and wonder how anyone ever hits anything with it.

Revolver grip compared to pistol grip. Note the obviously very different design philosophy between the two.

The natural grip angle of pistols causes them to point toward the target more easily and inherently than do revolvers. No pistol design has a better natural grip angle than Glock.

Compare revolver grips with pistol grips; lay one of each on a table and take a good look (one atop the other is best, but side by side will do). The semiauto's grip looks like the designer had defense tactics in mind, while the revolver's grip suggests it was designed for anything but. The pistol's grip is contoured for maximum comfort and control in the shooter's hand, but the revolver's is not. The revolver's is reminiscent of the seats in those wonderful classic roadsters from the 1920s: viciously uncomfortable and affording little support for control, but bearable. The pistol's grip, on the other hand, reminds one of the seats in a good-quality modern sports car: marvelously comfortable and affording excellent support for control.

It's no more correct to condemn revolver designers than it is to blame the designers of classic roadsters; they did the best they could with what they had. But modern design concepts have superseded the traditional and, at least where it counts (in fast cars and defense sidearms), the old ways just don't cut it any longer.

The way a pistol fits in the shooter's hand, the natural grip angle, and the manner in which it points, especially in relation to one's arm, all combine to permit faster target acquisition in high-stress situations. Semiauto shooters have better control generally, and especially on the first shot. Folks who have been shooting revolvers nearly always improve when trying pistols. Poor shooters' scores improve 30 to 40 percent, and average shooters' scores increase 20 to 30 percent.

Reloading

A major tactical advantage of pistols over revolvers is reloading speed. There's no way a revolver can be reloaded and returned to a gunfight faster than a semiauto. Don't tell me about fancy techniques, speedloaders, and the like until you've spent years on the tactical training range and seen it for yourself. Average reloading time (under stress) for a revolver is 9 to 15 seconds; for a pistol it's only 3 to 5.

Revolver diehards usually assert something such as, "If you can't handle whatever comes along with 6 rounds, you're in bigger trouble than 15 or more can get you out of." Whether that was ever true isn't the point; the point today is that we're seeing a huge increase in multiple assailants and criminals of all types equipped with high-capacity semiauto handguns. In its study of six thousand cases, the New York Police Department determined that more than 50 percent of the officers killed were alone but were attacked by more than one adversary (NYPD SOP9 Summary). The following appeared in the November 1990 issue of *Golden Gate Bridge*, an internal organ published by the California Highway Patrol: "Numerous incidents of armed drug traffickers found during routine traffic stops drove home the need for weapons with increased magazine capacity and reduced loading time.

Design Features

The tactical advantage of the semiautomatic pistol over the traditional .38 caliber and .357, combined with ballistic superiority, makes the auto a logical choice to replace our vintage revolvers."

If you don't believe reloading is important in gunfight situations, consider that since the 1850s, when police in America first began carrying sidearms (revolvers, of course), there have been many tragic officer deaths because revolvers are so awkward and slow to reload. But until relatively recently, tactics weren't taken so seriously as is necessary in today's society. The classic case still used as an example today is nearly forty years old.

In the 1950s, near Newhall in Southern California, a CHP officer involved in a gun battle with two people in a pickup truck was assassinated by one of the bad guys while taking cover behind his cruiser to reload his revolver.

Wondering why the officer had stopped shooting, the killer snuck around the cruiser for a peek. He spied the officer squatting there absorbed in reloading his revolver and carefully placing the empty cartridge cases in his pocket (that's what they were conditioned to do by training officers in those days), so he shot him in the head.

Reliability

One of the oldest and most tired of the revolver vs. pistol myths is that semiautos aren't as reliable as revolvers. Maybe that was once true, but things have changed. Modern pistols are designed for reliability, as is modern pistol ammunition.

Today's semiautomatic handguns are built with greater tolerances; they're able to function in the presence of dirt, sand, and other adverse conditions, sometimes even when revolvers can't. SIG-Sauer, for example, tested one of its pistols by fully immersing it in a container of mud and freezing it. After it was retrieved and the frozen mud chipped off, the pistol fired just fine. Some of the things Glocks have been subjected to are astounding, but their reliability continues to prove even more so. Remember the Miami PD tests discussed in Chapter 2? They consisted of such things as throwing and dropping a Model 17 on steel and concrete from heights up to 60 feet, submerging it in saltwater for fifty hours, and firing 1,000 rounds through it in forty-five minutes. The FBI threw a loaded (with live ammunition) Model 17 out of a speeding car on a runway at Andrews Air Force Base, and the Georgia Highway Patrol dropped one out of a patrol helicopter several times from about 400 feet. No problem—the guns worked just fine after each test.

One of the very important things about semiautomatic handguns is that even if one does malfunction, chances are a properly trained operator will be able to clear it and return it to service fast enough to save his or her life. (See Chapter 14, "Operational Advantages," for more on how to deal with malfunctions in tactical situations.) When a revolver malfunctions it usually means a trip to the gunsmith.

Maintenance

Modern pistols require less routine maintenance than revolvers do. I know, according to firearms lore such a claim is sacrilege, but it's true. Today's high-tech semiautos actually require less time and energy to maintain than do revolvers, which don't enjoy the technological advances so common in new pistols.

Many of those advances reduce the necessity for cleaning and other routine maintenance chores. Additionally, modern pistols are far easier and faster to "take down" for cleaning and maintenance than are older versions. Indeed, most modern pistols can be cleaned faster than revolvers can. And as for maintenance, revolvers may appear simpler at first glance, but in reality they're every bit as complex as pistols—and more so than some, such as Glocks.

Design Features

Revolvers and American Police

That American police so long eschewed semiautomatics is curious because they're so strongly influenced by the military. Except for the British (who followed their military in abandoning the .455 Webley revolver in favor of the Browning Hi-Power in the 1950s), virtually all European police, indeed, police worldwide, have long used pistols.

The European fervor for pistols is exemplified by what happened in Germany following World War II. After Germany's surrender on 6 May 1945, its military was disbanded and the police were outfitted with Model 10 M&Ps and other Smith & Wesson revolvers. The German police were unhappy about this but could do nothing until the occupation ended in 1951. As soon as Conrad Adenauer's new government began operating, the German police sought to get rid of their revolvers. They couldn't afford anything better than cheap Spanish semiautomatics, but to them that was better even than good quality Smith & Wesson revolvers, so they made the change.

But despite all that, American police (and as a result of their influence, much of the American populace) held steadfastly to revolvers. Being out of step with the rest of the world, flying in the face of American military tradition, and even receiving considerable pressure from the rank and file failed to sway police chiefs and administrators. There was no valid reason for their refusal to switch, but they offered weak arguments such as: changing to pistols will result in a hodge-podge of weaponry among police, leading to tactical and financial disaster for departments. This was, of course, unadulterated crap. If departments could standardize types and models of revolvers, they could do the same with pistols, just as the military had.

Revolvers and the FBI

The FBI, like so many other federal agencies and the vast majority of police departments, had used revolvers since its inception. That is, until 11 April 1986, when Michael Platt and Edward Matix left so many FBI agents lying dead and wounded on Miami's S.W. 82nd Avenue, thereby setting into motion a course of events that would forever change the way law enforcement viewed its sidearms.

In the aftermath of that tragedy, many things came to light, and among them were some facts about revolvers. For example, none of the FBI agents who'd shot their revolvers dry were able to reload them successfully and continue shooting. Gordon McNeill, supervisory special agent, discovered something dreadful during the heat of battle. After shooting his revolver dry he hunkered down behind a car to reload. Knowing Platt was on the other side with a Ruger Mini-14 rifle, and fearing he'd be killed if he didn't get his revolver back into service very quickly, McNeill decided there was time to load only two of the four rounds he had in his hand into the six empty chambers. Much to his horror, he realized that he couldn't remember which way the cylinder of his revolver turned and, as he said later, "You certainly don't want to hit on four empties if you only get two in there." McNeill later said that during all this he'd had "great difficulty" trying to reload his revolver; his right hand was wounded and there was blood and bone in the open cylinder.

Another agent who was there, Ron Riser, emptied his Smith & Wesson Model 459 semiautomatic and "reached for the nearest thing with bullets in it." That happened to be his Smith & Wesson Model 60 revolver carried in an ankle holster. He fired one or two rounds with it and "realized it just wasn't going to cut it." So he reloaded his semiautomatic Model 459 and continued firing.

Design Features

Law Enforcement Finally Sees the Light

Something happened in the 1980s. It may have been the military's change to a wondernine, the Beretta M9/92F. It may have been the FBI's adoption of semiautos following the Miami disaster. It may have been that so many cops were outgunned and getting slaughtered on the streets fighting drug-related crime. Or it may have been some combination of those and other factors. It really doesn't matter why. What matters is that it finally happened: police departments throughout America began replacing their revolvers with pistols.

Now the military has a high-tech pistol, FBI agents use pistols, and police are switching to pistols in droves. Those who bristle at suggestions of pistol tactical superiority over revolvers are finding themselves in the minority.

Glock Tactical Advantages

Glock pistols are tactically advantageous in many ways. Some advantages come in the form of operational techniques and related benefits not available in other pistols, and others are purely the result of serendipitous design. Let's look at the latter.

Natural Grip Angle
Even among superior pistols, Glock's ergonomically designed grip angle seems to be the best; it's very natural and comfortable for most people. As Ayoob pointed out in *Guns*, Glock's grip angle is quite "Luger-like"—something that facilitates natural pointing "like an extension of your hand."

It's true. A Glock feels good in most people's hands. And it points so naturally that most people do remarkably well right from the start. I've seen many new shooters fire their very first shot from a Glock at the beginning of a class, and half a day and 300 rounds later they're outshooting most experienced students who are using other guns. A good deal of the reason they're able to do that is the Glock's natural grip angle.

Low Bore Axis

At least as important as natural grip angle is the Glock's low bore axis. This is important because a low bore axis reduces muzzle flip; therefore, comfort and controllability are increased while perceived (felt) recoil is reduced.

The bore is the hole down the barrel through which bullets travel immediately after being fired from the ammunition cartridge. The end of the bore closest to the shooter is the breech end, where the firing chamber is located; the other end of the bore is the muzzle, the business end. If you traced the midline of a bullet's path as it left the firing chamber and sped down the barrel and out the muzzle, that line would describe the bore axis. A low bore axis is closer to the grip than a high bore axis. The recurve is the upper, rearward curving part of the grip into which the web of the shooter's hand fits.

The distance from the midpoint of the recurve to the bore axis on a SIG-Sauer P220/226 is 2 inches; that distance on a Smith & Wesson Model 5944 is 1.75 inches. On a Glock Model 19 it's only 1.25 inches. That may seem inconsequential, but from a biotechnological perspective it's rather significant, and the benefits are quite apparent, especially to shooters with little or no experience.

Less distance between the bore axis and the recurve means the upward force vector produced when a round is fired works on the shooter's hand with less magnitude. In other words, there is less tendency to flip muzzle up. This makes the pistol easier to handle and more comfortable to shoot.

Because muzzle flip is reduced, the pistols seems to be hitting the shooter's hand with less force. Actually, all else being equal, less muzzle flip seems to reduce recoil for two reasons: 1) recoil force is distributed more evenly throughout the area of contact between the pistol and the shooter's hand, and 2) more recoil force is imparted to less pressure-sensitive portions of the shooter's hand. Conversely, when a pistol flips muzzle up during recoil, much of its force is concentrated in the web of the shooter's hand. This causes whatever recoil force there is to feel greater than if it were spread throughout the shooter's palm, simply because force concentrated in a smaller area feels stronger than when the same amount of force is spread over a larger area. Also, when most of that force is concentrated in the hand's web, a particularly sensitive area compared to the palm, it feels stronger yet.

Low Felt Recoil

Comfort when shooting is tactically important to everyone (even the "tough guys" who refuse to admit to any discomfort), but it is of particular importance to new and/or inexperienced shooters. Discomfort is a major distraction, and in a genuine life-or-death shooting situation, such unnecessary distractions are highly undesirable.

A significant factor affecting comfort is "felt recoil"—the force perceived in one's hand during firing. It isn't how much actual recoil a gun generates, it's how it feels in your hand. Two pistols that generate exactly the same actual recoil might have quite different felt recoil.

Grip Size and Shape

Several factors affect felt recoil (actual recoil, bore axis height, etc.), but nothing has greater effect than the size and shape of the grip. Obviously, a grip design that distributes recoil over a larger surface area feels "softer" in one's hand. Look at the grip, especially the backstrap, of any handgun. Regardless of what type of gun or how the grip is designed, imagine a very sharp ridge running from top to bottom along the very back of the gun, where it would be right in the palm of your shooting hand. Ouch! Now, in your mind, restore the backstrap to its original condition. See how much softer it will feel during firing?

The feel of Glock grips appeals to a great many people. It's common to hear expressions of surprise among new shooters who expected firing to be uncomfortable. And you know how converts are: experienced shooters who become Glock devotees—and there's an amazing and continually expanding hoard of them—don't fall in love with these pistols because they're uncomfortable.

Polymer Frame

Possibly even more important to shooting comfort is yet another of Glock pistols' unique features: the polymer frame. Yes, it is plastic. And among the definitions of the word "plastic" are: ductile, elastic, flexible, pliant. During firing, the receivers of Glock pistols actually flex. This causes them to absorb actual recoil and impart it to the shooter's hand differently than would a rigid receiver. In other words, the flexible receiver contributes to reduced felt recoil.

Action Balance

How the action—more specifically, the slide—is balanced greatly affects felt recoil. Superficially, slide function during the firing cycle of a recoil-operated pistol is simple: recoil force from ammunition discharge drives the slide rearward, compressing the recoil spring; then the slide is propelled forward by the expansion force of the compressed recoil spring.

In a perfect world, pistol slides would have enough recoil energy to extract and eject cartridge cases and reach the rear slide stop, achieving the full extent of their rearward travel just as the last bit of recoil energy was depleted. But it's not a perfect world, and pistol slides don't snuggle up to rear stops, barely kiss them, and gently begin the return trip back into battery.

It's theoretically possible to balance a pistol's action perfectly, but it would have to be done for one specific ammunition cartridge. Any variables would disturb the balance, including deviations in performance in the specific cartridge for which the pistol was balanced.

If ammunition more powerful than that for which the pistol was balanced is used, the slide will batter the receiver each and every firing cycle, eventually leading to damage and even the possibility of catastrophic failure. On the other hand, if ammunition less powerful than that for which the pistol was balanced is used, recoil energy insufficient to fully compress the recoil spring will result in the slide failing to reach the rear slide stop.

Incomplete slide cycling results in such things as failures to eject, also known as "stovepipes" (see the section on stoppages in Chapter 14). Also, a slide that starts forward before completing its rearward travel will be unable to strip a fresh round from the magazine and feed it into the firing chamber.

Most manufacturers attempt to resolve the dilemma of slide balance by compromising, and you know what that means: everything is resolved with mediocrity, nothing with brilliance.

Accepting mediocrity, most pistol manufacturers skew the compromise toward operational reliability. In other words, they build their guns to function reliably with less powerful ammunition. While such a compromised pistol will function with a wider range of ammunition, the necessarily weaker recoil spring will permit slide-battering when more powerful ammunition is used. Most modern pistols can withstand pounding of this type without significant damage, at least for a while, but it does wreak havoc on felt recoil. Yep, most pistols hit your hand pretty hard, partly because a recoil spring weak enough to permit complete slide cycling with lower-power ammunition lets the slide slam against the rear stop and in turn lets the gun slam into your hand.

Glock's pistol design needs far less compromise to achieve low felt recoil along with functional reliability throughout a wide range of ammunition performance. In addition to low felt recoil inherent in Glock pistols by virtue of the low bore axis, grip shape, and polymer receiver, Glock has managed to balance the slide so it functions reliably throughout a broad range of ammunition performance.

Usually pistols with delicately balanced slides are fairly temperamental and function consistently only when everything's just right. Say what you will about Glock pistols, but they can hardly be called delicate or temperamental. On the contrary, Glocks are known to be tough guns that eagerly digest just about any kind of ammunition and function reliably in all sorts of conditions and situations. As with any pistol, however, there are limitations to this. Glocks are not perfect—just better than other pistols. (See Chapter 14 for operational consequences relating to slide balancing.)

Magazines

Any tactically oriented, in-depth discussion of Glock pistols eventually turns to magazines, specifically Glock magazines' tendency to not drop free from the pistol when released. While it is true that early Glock magazines did have some problems, the fact that they don't drop free was not (at least according to Glock) among them. They were designed to not drop free for a very specific reason, and the design is not likely to be changed. (For more about this, see Chapter 14, "Operational Advantages.")

Bodies and Floorplates

Early Glock magazine bodies were made from more pliable polymer, whereas later ones are made from a formulation that produces more rigid polymer. The older, more pliant magazine bodies sometimes deformed when warm, thus permitting the floorplate to pop off when the magazine was dropped, especially if it was more than about 50-percent filled. While rarely a tactical liability, watching helplessly as one's magazine springs open upon hitting the ground, disgorging live rounds willy-nilly in all directions tended to try even the most tolerant person's patience. This never happens with new Glock magazines.

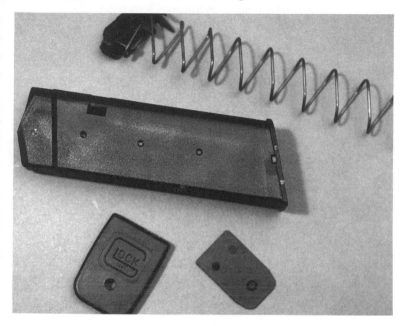

The five components of a current-production Model 23 .40 S&W magazine. Top to bottom: magazine spring and magazine follower, magazine body, magazine floorplate, subfloorplate.

In fact, the more rigid new Glock magazine bodies are so much less malleable that they're significantly more difficult to dismantle intentionally. To disassemble the older magazines it was necessary only to press inward on the body near the floorplate, where the two little retaining tabs are located. Now, however, so much more pressure is required to overcome the new polymer's rigidity that some people can't do it manually, and others can do it only with extreme difficulty. And so far we're talking only about the 9mm magazines.

The 10mm, .40 S&W, and .45 ACP magazines are even more difficult to disassemble. Not only are the magazine bodies for these calibers made with the more rigid polymer, they all share a single significant difference from the original 9mm magazine design: there is a subfloorplate between the magazine spring and the floorplate with a small post on the underside. That post fits into a corresponding hole in the floorplate. When assembled, the magazine spring presses the subfloorplate hard against the inside of the floorplate, thus making the post inside the floorplate hole prevent the floorplate from sliding off the magazine body.

Various magazine floorplates compared. Left to right: Model 21 .45 ACP, Model 22 .40 S&W, very early Model 23 .40 S&W (before subfloorplate was included), and Model 17 9mm.

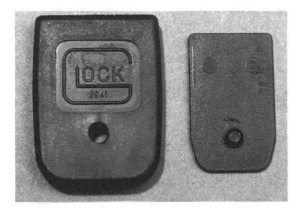

A current-production Model 23 .40 S&W floorplate and subfloorplate with hole and corresponding post.

This is good in all respects except for magazine disassembly. The already difficult-to-remove floorplate from the already difficult-to-squeeze magazine body becomes even more difficult to deal with because the subfloorplate's little post must be depressed sufficiently to release the floorplate, allowing it to slide off the magazine body when the latter is squeezed sufficiently so its two little tabs clear the floorplate's corresponding notches. If you think that's a mouthful to say, just try to do it. It takes three hands, plus two exceptionally strong digits with rather pain-resistant tips.

Old-style magazine (left) compared to newer version (right). Note straight shoulder of old-style compared to improved angled rear portion of the newer magazine.

The new magazines also differ in another way. The magazine bodies are slightly narrower at the top 1/2 inch or so than they are lower down. In fact, where the main body has parallel sides, the top 1/2 inch is not only a little narrower, it's also slightly tapered, being about 1/4 inch narrower than the main body at the lips and widening to only about 1/8 inch narrower about 1/2 inch down. About 1/2 inch down from the top there's a small ridge, or shoulder, on each side of the magazine body, where the narrower tapered top part meets the parallel-sided main body. The ridges run parallel to the floorplate.

On the old-style magazines these ridges were completely straight on both sides, but on the new-style magazines only the ridge on the right side is. On the left side the ridge is straight from the front corner until a point just slightly more than 1/2 inch from the back corner. At that point the little ridge angles up just a bit on the 9mm and .40 S&W magazines. On the .45 ACP and 10mm magazines it remains straight, but the shoulder is molded more like a flat shelf, whereas the ridge forward of that is angled downward.

The purpose of this change is a very important one indeed. It corrects a problem that existed with the older magazines: excessive wear on the magazine catch notch located on the right side of the magazine body. Other than the magazine catch notch, the only thing that prevents overinsertion of the older-style magazines is the floorplate contacting the bottom edges of the magazine well. The already quite flexible polymer is also quite thin there and was not designed to be a magazine stop; thus, it does a poor job of it. As a result, it is common to see old-style magazines with excessive wear on the bottom edge of the magazine catch notch.

Contemporaneously with production of the improved magazines, Glock added a small polygon of polymer at the very top of the magazine well on the left side, just behind the slide-stop lever and just forward of the ejector. It is designed to meet the new-style magazines' little shoulder and provide a positive stop (upper limit of travel) for magazines. This eliminates any wear and tear on the magazine catch notch and assures proper positioning and seating of magazines in the pistol.

Followers

The magazine followers have also been improved on new magazines. The older followers had a rectangular extension from the left front corner. This small protrusion was designed to contact and apply upward pressure on a little metal tab coming off the slide-stop lever. Such contact only occurs when the magazine is empty; the follower is below any ammunition rounds in the magazine so it can't make contact with the slide-stop lever unless there are no rounds. But when the magazine is empty, the follower rises all the way to the top, and the little extension pushes up on the slide-stop lever's little tab. This causes the slide-stop lever, normally spring-loaded in the down position, to engage the notch on the slide, holding it open after the last round is fired.

The little extension on the old style magazine follower used to wear down with use and eventually would fail to push up sufficiently on the slide-stop lever to engage the slide and hold it open after the last round was fired. A common fix is to slightly bend the slide-stop lever's little tab down to compensate for the worn away extension on the follower. This works only for a while, until the follower wears down more. Eventually the slide-stop lever's tab will have been bent so

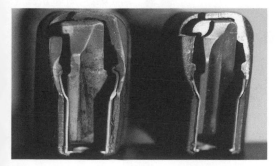

much that it can no longer reach the worn down follower extension.

Old-style magazine follower (left) compared to new design (right).

221

The new followers are redesigned so the problem no longer exists. Instead of a rectangular extension that is the same height as the leading edge of the follower, the new design incorporates a rounded extension that's slightly lower than the follower's leading edge. This design change, along with the same tougher polymer as used in the new magazine bodies, effectively prevents follower erosion and resultant failure to lock open the slide after the last round has been fired.

Magazine Catch

Glock pistols' magazine catch, called a magazine release by some, is nothing more than an L-shaped polymer piece with some ridges, a depression, and a notch molded into it. The catch fits into place from the receiver's right side, the ridged straight end protruding slightly just behind the trigger guard on the left side and the curved end flush with the grip in the corresponding location on the right side.

Magazine catch notch of older-style magazine. Note damage to top (left in photo) and bottom (right in photo) edges, caused by the lack of any other insertion-depth-limiting feature. Damage of this type no longer occurs on newer magazines with angled rear shoulder portion to limit depth of insertion.

Many people complain that they are unable to reach the magazine catch with their right thumb (assuming a right-handed shooter) when holding the pistol in the normal shooting grip. To that Glock says: "Wunderbar!"

Gaston Glock designed the magazine catch that way on purpose so it wouldn't be activated unintentionally at some inauspicious moment, causing the pistol operator great embarrassment, to say nothing of exposing him or her to potentially more grievous harm.

There is a tactical procedure to cope with this (see Chapter 14, "Operational Advantages") and, for those who simply must have an easier-to-reach catch, a mechanical fix (see Chapter 15, "Accessories and Special Stuff.")

• • • • •

The design features that many people believe make Glock pistols tactically superior among modern high-tech law enforcement/defense handguns are only part of the story. The numerous operational advantages are delineated in the following chapter.

CHAPTER 14
Operational Advantages

he previous chapter begins by mentioning the so-called "fundamental notion" that a semiautomatic handgun (pistol) is tactically superior to a revolver. In this chapter we'll explore that a little more fully and take a good look at some of the reasons it's true. We'll also look at some of the operational features that give the individual shooting a Glock the edge in tactical situations. But first, some basic information.

Law Enforcement Studies

In a recent study (NYC SOP9) that analyzed six thousand cases in the department, the New York Police Department revealed that 49 officers were killed by assailants, another 256 were shot and wounded, and yet another 256 were stabbed and wounded. A summary of the study brings many important facts to light. Some bear directly on the issue of pistol superiority over revolvers in tactical situations. For example, in more than 50 percent of the cases in which an officer was killed, the officer was alone and there was more than one attacker. More facts:

1) Surprise was a significant factor in 70 percent of the cases where injury or death occurred—even when the officer knew

beforehand that some greater-than-usual danger existed (e.g., situations such as responding to a felony in progress, shots-fired or man-with-a-gun calls, or suspicious and/or disorderly person calls). Moreover, many situations wherein there was a rapid threat escalation immediately prior to the death or injury were often considered routine (e.g., traffic stops and guarding or transporting prisoners and/or emotionally disturbed persons).

2) Lighting was also a factor. In 65 to 75 percent of the incidents in which officers used their firearms, the area was poorly lit, although none occurred in total darkness. Virtually no officers used flashlights in conjunction with their firearms in order to facilitate target identification or shot placement.

3) Distance was a very significant factor. Included in the SOP9 study were reports compiled by NYPD from September 1854 through December 1979. During that period, 254 officers were killed in armed encounters. Of the 254, an astounding 229 (90 percent) were killed by an adversary who stood at a distance of 5 yards or less! Here's the breakdown:

NYPD Report: Officers Killed 1854-1979

Assailant's Distance	Number of Officers	Percent
0 to 3 feet	86	34
3 to 6 feet	119	47
6 to 15 feet	24	9
15 to 25 feet	12	5
125 feet (sniper)	1	0
Undetermined dist.	12	5
Totals	**254**	**100**

The FBI "Uniform Crime Reports" statistics for the years 1974 through 1983 correlate closely with NYPD's survey:

FBI "Uniform Crime Reports"
Officers Killed 1974-1983

Assailant's Distance	Officers Killed	Percent
0 to 5 feet	494	51
6 to 10 feet	192	20
11 to 20 feet	152	16
21 to 50 feet	66	7
More than 50 feet	56	6
Totals	**960**	**100**

Combining the FBI's and NYPD's numbers, the average distance of armed encounters is six to seven feet, and the average time is 3.2 seconds.

NYPD's study tells us that surprise, lighting, and distance are significant factors, and the FBI's statistics ratify the distance factor. The averages confirm that close assailants are a major factor and explicitly state that time is crucial.

In fact, the factors of surprise, lighting, and distance all equate to time in tactical situations. Any well-trained, streetwise, tactically capable individual will tell you that nothing is more important than time during a deadly encounter. How does the time factor relate to the alleged tactical superiority of pistols over revolvers? Is a pistol any faster than a revolver? Let's check it out.

Time and Triggers

There are essentially four action types: 1) single-action-only, 2) double-action-only, 3) selective double-action (double action first shot, single action thereafter, i.e., pistols with decocking levers), and 4) Glock Safe Action. Police-style revolvers are generally referred to as double-action-only, but actually, most can be hand-cocked to single-action mode.

Single-action-only pistols are the granddaddies of

defense pistols. Because they can be fired only in single-action mode (which means they have light triggers with little movement required to discharge the weapon), they always have an affirmative safety device. Deployment is fast (if the operator is well-trained), but manipulation of both the safety and trigger is required to get the first shot off.

Double-action-only pistols generally do not have affirmative safeties and in that respect are readily deployable. Because of their relatively heavy triggers with long pulls required, however, it's common for shooters to take longer than necessary to get off the first shot and/or to miss the first shot.

Selective double-action pistols are those with hammers that cock each time the slide goes to the rear, whether powered by the shooter's hand (as when chambering the first round) or by normal cycling during firing. This type of pistol comes equipped with a decocking lever instead of an affirmative safety. Rather than engaging a safety device after chambering the first round (to guard against the short, light trigger that comes with single-action mode), the operator lowers the hammer (using the decocking lever) to return the pistol to double-action mode (long, hard trigger). Just as with double-action-only pistols, selective double-action guns tend to produce slower deployment times and more misses on the first shot. But even worse than double-action-only pistols, selective double-action ones revert to single-action mode on the second and subsequent shots (unless the operator takes the time to lower the hammer with the decocking lever). This means that not only is there significant likelihood of missing the first shot, it's at least as likely that the second will go awry as well.

Police-style revolvers are very much like double-action-only pistols (and they are generally referred to as such, although most can be hand-cocked to single-action mode) insofar as deployment speed and first-shot accuracy are concerned. Some believe them to be slightly worse, but others disagree. It makes little difference, as both are relatively slow and difficult by comparison to more highly evolved guns.

Glock Safe Action solves virtually all of the above problems. According to the BATF, Glock pistols are double-action-only because they require the same trigger force and travel each and every time a shot is fired. But Glock Safe Action differs from the trigger-action of ordinary double-action-only pistols because not only is the trigger exactly the same for every pull, but trigger force and travel better facilitate rapid deployment and effective first-shot placement.

Glock's Fast Trigger

Glock's Safe Action facilitates rapid deployment and effective first-shot placement because there are no flip-flap levers or other dealies to mess with—when it's time, one simply draws, aims, and fires a Glock pistol. Fast and effective.

In these times of multiple adversaries and other tactical exigencies, the slow old six-shooters just aren't able to cut the mustard. As often as not, several shots must be fired to deal with a threat effectively. That's why the majority of police firearms trainers who aren't limited by antiquated low-capacity, low-technology weapons all teach double- and triple-tap techniques. And believe me, when the chips are down and the only way to get out is to fire multiple shots, there's no handgun better than a Glock.

Glock triggers have about 4/10 inch of slack—relatively unrestricted rearward travel—before significant resistance is encountered. Once resistance is encountered (this means the rear extension of the trigger bar has contacted the connector's angled ramp—see Chapter 11 for more on this), the trigger requires only about 1/8 inch of additional rearward travel in order to discharge the weapon. That's dandy, but what about double- and triple-taps?

Well, not only do Glocks require astonishingly little

trigger travel to fire, the forward travel to reset the trigger is just as amazingly short—about 1/8 inch. You can try this on your own Glock.

Glock Model 17 with trigger in full forward position.

Glock Model 17 with trigger fully pressed to the rear.

CAUTION: Verify and reverify that your pistol is unloaded before proceeding. Once you are certain the pistol is empty, pull the trigger and hold it back. Still holding it, cycle the slide. Now, slowly and carefully allow the trigger to move forward. When it clicks, the trigger is reset and ready to fire again.

This is the position in which all of the slack has been removed during trigger actuation. It's also the trigger reset point after firing. Note how little forward movement is required to reset the trigger, a distinct tactical advantage during rapid-fire or double tap operations.

Glock's trigger mechanism permits faster multiple shots than any other handgun on the market. But to take full advantage of this remarkable design, one must learn the proper technique, then reinforce it with practice from time to time. It's really very easy: under suitable firing range conditions, fire the first shot, then release the trigger only to the reset point (about 1/8 inch), then fire another shot. Repeat as necessary. With a little practice you'll be able to empty a magazine so fast you won't believe it.

So if surprise, poor lighting, and/or a very close assailant demand rapid deployment and effective shot placement under adverse conditions, Glock pistols rise to the occasion. And again, when multiple adversaries or other dire circumstances require a series of fast, effective shots, Glock pistols perform better than all others.

Stoppages

Some call them failures to fire; to others they're jams or malfunctions. Perhaps it doesn't matter what you call them, but why not strive for precision? Because sometimes such things are caused by the gun, other times by the ammunition, and still others by the operator, if they're to be lumped together, why not use a label that applies to them all? That's only one reason some of us prefer the term "stoppage." The other, more tactically significant, is that adverse conditioning, no matter how subtle, is considered highly undesirable by first-rate firearms and tactics trainers. In this case, using a generic label that doesn't subtly predispose the operator toward any particular diagnosis could save valuable time in a high-stress situation.

The firing cycle of a semiautomatic handgun is: feed, fire, extract, and eject. Stoppages can occur in any phase of the cycle and are classified as: 1) failures to feed/fire, 2) failures to extract, and 3) failures to eject.

Failures to Feed

Causes of failures to feed (failures to completely and properly chamber a round of ammunition) can be as simple as unavailable ammunition due to an improperly seated, malfunctioning, missing, or empty magazine. Failures to feed can also result from deformed, incorrectly sized, or really grungy ammunition that simply will not fit into the chamber; or a very cruddy pistol with so much dirt in critical places that the slide can't go into battery completely.

A failure to feed viewed through the ejection port. Note that the round is jammed at a slight angle, as it is partially out of the magazine and into the chamber.

A slide fully in battery.

A slightly out-of-battery slide. Compare it to the previous photograph: note by the forward and rear edges that it's not quite all the way forward (into battery). Also, notice the rear of the barrel hasn't come all the way up to lock against the breechface, as can be seen by the top of the firing chamber not being flush with the slide top, as it is in the previous photograph.

Possibly the most common reason for failures to feed is an improperly seated magazine. If the magazine isn't properly seated, the slide cannot strip the top round from the magazine and deliver it into the chamber.

Glock magazines tend to fit rather tightly in the magazine well, especially when full. Remember the CHP report (Chapter 4) that focused so heavily on Glock magazines' tendency to not fall free when released? Well, sometimes they don't insert as easily as do those of other pistols either. Regardless of why Glock magazines tend to fit more snugly than most people are used to, it's important to remember that because they do, they must be inserted with conviction to ensure proper seating.

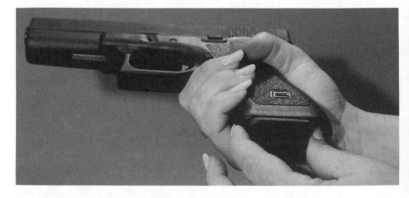

The correct manner in which to grasp a magazine for tugging to determine whether or not it is fully seated and locked. Note how the cut in the front strap and the space between the magazine and the back strap facilitate a firm grasp of the magazine.

When inserting a Glock magazine under normal, non-stress conditions, it's necessary to listen/feel for the "click" as the magazine catch snaps into its notch. The "click" indicates the magazine is fully seated. A second, entirely tactile check is to feel the curved portion of the magazine catch on the grip's right side, just behind the trigger guard. If it's not flush, the magazine isn't fully seated. The best verification of proper magazine seating, however, is to grasp the floorplate with your thumb and forefinger and give a little tug. This can be done whether the pistol is in your hand or holstered.

A damaged magazine can cause a failure to feed as well. Especially with older Glock magazines, force-loading an extra round can cause the magazine tube to bulge. This, in turn, can cause several problems, including but not limited to: the follower and/or spring failing to exert proper upward pressure on the ammunition, rounds in the magazine losing their characteristic "zig-zag" relationship to one another, the magazine lips' separation going out-of-limits, etc. Any or all of these can result in ammunition failing to feed properly, even when the magazine is seated correctly.

Obviously, failing to insert a magazine—or inserting an empty magazine—will deprive your Glock of any chance whatsoever to chamber and fire a round of ammunition. Fortunately, such lapses are far less common than failures to seat the magazine properly, but they do happen.

For a dirt-caused stoppage, the obvious remedy is ultimately to remove the dirt. Absent time-based exigencies, fieldstripping and thorough cleaning are recommended. In tactical situations, however, where there is time pressure, the tendency when experiencing a failure to feed in which the slide hasn't gone completely into battery (a most common condition in dirt-caused feed failures) is to attempt to force the slide the rest of the way. This temptation should be resisted.

Forcing an out-of-battery slide risks jamming a dirty, deformed, or otherwise faulty round of ammunition into the firing chamber. If it wouldn't fully chamber during normal slide cycling, forcing it without correcting the problem can cause a round to lodge so tenaciously that, at the very least, precious time will be lost clearing it. And it could be worse; it's possible that a seriously stuck round could require pistol disassembly for removal.

Sometimes a slide fails to go into battery completely

for reasons other than the above. Such things as a little dirt on the rails or elsewhere, a weak recoil spring, or something else fairly innocuous (such as a finger or thumb riding the slide) can be the culprits.

Some tactical trainers and others are of the opinion that in such cases, a little gentle forward pressure on the back of the slide is appropriate. The theory is that if the out-of-battery condition can be corrected by pushing the slide closed, it is best to try it because, if it works, it will put the pistol back in service faster than any other attempted remedy. While that's accurate for conditions that will allow such correction, the obvious downside is the possibility of really jamming up the gun, so that considerably more time is required to get it back in operating condition.

It's a tactical decision everyone must make for himself. My only caution for those opting for the "slide push" remedy would be to use only a very small amount of force. If the technique won't work with just a little pressure, chances are that tap-rack-bang (see p. 244) is more appropriate, and more likely to clear the stoppage faster than anything else at that point.

Barrel obstructions can also cause a round of ammunition not to chamber completely, leaving the slide out of battery. The most common cause is a bullet stuck in the pipe as the result of a squib load (a cartridge with no—or very little—powder that generated only enough power to push the bullet out of the case and lodge it in the barrel).

Whenever possible during rapid firing, listen/feel for any unusual or abnormal discharges. If anything suspicious is perceived, immediately cease firing. While Glock barrels are far stronger than those of other pistols, it is still possible for damage to occur if a bullet is fired into an obstructed barrel.

Glock barrels are extremely strong. For example, the 9mm barrels can safely handle 43,500 psi (pounds per square inch) chamber pressure. That's impressive, considering that SAAMI (Sporting Arms and Ammunition Manufacturers' Institute) specifications call for a maximum pressure of 30,457 psi, and NATO (North Atlantic Treaty Organization) specifies an upper pressure limit of 37,709 psi.

Failures to Fire

A failure to fire at a crucial moment can cause your pistol to emit the loudest sound in the world—in the case of a Glock, a slightly metallic, rather innocuous "snap" immediately after you pressed the trigger and just when you expected to hear a loud bang.

If bad ammunition causes a failure to fire, it's either a primer or powder problem. More than likely it's the primer, as powder rarely causes a failure to fire in anything except handloads, and you shouldn't be using them for defense anyway.

Primer problems can result from a high, inverted, or missing primer. Missing primers are uncommon, inverted ones less so; high primers are seen more than the others. In nonstress situations you can carefully remove a round that was chambered properly but failed to fire (wait twenty to thirty seconds, then remove following the manual extraction procedure described below) and look at the primer. If there's a dimple in the primer, that means the firing pin struck but failed to detonate it, most likely because the primer wasn't fully seated. When the firing pin struck, all it did was fully seat the primer, dimpling it, but not imparting sufficient force to set it off.

Manual Extraction Procedure

Some Glock trainers and others worry that the primer of a live round being manually ejected from the chamber could contact the ejector and detonate it. Because of this, these folks urge operators of Glock pistols to avoid catching extracted rounds in their hands.

This is sound advice under tactically exigent conditions when time is the most precious commodity. At such times the slide should be moved smartly rearward to the stops and the ejected round allowed to fall freely to the ground.

Whenever there is no time pressure, however, manual extraction need not be done so crudely and forcefully. Without the excuse of tactical pressure, it's better not to fling live rounds from the chamber to the ground. Inevitably they hide (sometimes in plain sight), causing one or more people to spend several minutes imitating ostriches. While this may be amusing to see, it isn't the safest thing to do at a gun-firing place.

Whenever there is no urgency, the best way to manually extract a round from the chamber of a pistol is to:

1. Hold the gun normally with the gun hand.
2. Place the nongun hand over the ejection port.
3. Rotate the gun so the ejection port faces the ground.
4. Slowly and gently move the slide rearward (CAVEAT: if any resistance is felt, immediately cease rearward slide movement and remove your hand from the ejection port).
5. Either lock the slide open or return it to battery.

Two Feed/Fire Failures

Failures to feed and/or fire—mostly caused by the things mentioned above—are seen fairly often by trainers. But occasionally something unusual comes along. The following are two such examples (one of each type of failure) from recent personal experience.

Failure to fire: While closely observing the hands of a female student firing a Glock Model 19 during a rapid-fire exercise in a basic threat-management class, I heard the sound of an abnormal discharge accompanied by the emission of a small puff of white smoke from the ejection port. The student was prevented from actuating the trigger again after the peculiar sight and sound occurred. Following an appropriate period of waiting to ensure there was no hangfire and that the offending round would not go off, we emptied the chamber and examined the ejected cartridge.

Usually when a squib load occurs, the bullet is expelled from the casing and lodges somewhere in the barrel, often just beyond or very near to the firing chamber. This time, however, we did not find the expected empty case that results when such things happen. Instead, we found that the bullet was still in place, but the primer had been blown out and was missing. There was unburnt gunpowder in the case; it poured from the primer hole when the case was held upright.

This was factory ammunition from Winchester. We inspected all remaining rounds and found them in perfect condition; indeed, the student fired them all without mishap later in the day. The exact cause of this problem is uncertain, but we do know detonation of some sort occurred with sufficient force to unlock the action enough to allow the small puff of white smoke to escape. We also know that little or no pressure rise occurred inside the case because the bullet was not dislodged.

In light of those facts, and because there was considerable unburnt powder in the case, it is likely that the round had an inverted primer which detonated when struck by the firing pin, producing enough force backwards (toward the rear of the pistol, directly against the breechface) to open the action slightly. But because the primer had been installed backwards, the flash hole (between the primer pocket and the gunpowder reservoir) was sealed, so no part of the primer's flame could reach the gunpowder.

Failure to feed: During a Glock Tactical Operations training class, a federal officer firing his off-duty Model 23 experienced a series of failures to feed. The first occurred late in the day during a move-and-shoot exercise. The student completed the exercise after promptly clearing the stoppage (the slide was not all the way in battery) using the tap-rack-bang procedure (see p. 244).

The pistol and ejected round (the one that didn't make it all the way into the chamber) were superficially inspected, but nothing was found that would have caused the out-of-battery condition. More attempts to fire the Model 23 resulted in several similar stoppages. The slide was removed and the receiver's rails were cleaned with Prolix, but stoppages continued after reassembly.

It was a perplexing problem. Other than improper or filthy ammunition, an excessively dirty pistol (and Glocks have to be astoundingly dirty before they'll malfunction), a faulty recoil spring, or an obstructed chamber or barrel—all of which were checked for and determined to not be factors—there are very few things that can cause a Glock pistol's slide not to go all the way into battery. Actually, anything that interferes with free slide movement can do it, including the shooter's thumb or fingers "riding" the slide. This occurs when a portion of the shooter's hand, usually a thumb or finger, contacts the slide as it moves back and forth, causing friction so subtle the shooter usually isn't even aware it's happening. Close observation of the officer during firing, however, eliminated this as a possible cause.

A thorough inspection finally disclosed the problem: it was not a failure of the pistol after all. The officer had night sights installed by someone who was not a factory-certified Glock armorer. During installation—probably because a tool specially made by the factory and available only from them was not used to secure the front sight—the retaining bolt's head split. A small portion of the broken head bent just enough to interfere with the slide assembly just before it could go completely into battery. Once the offending part was removed, the Model 23 functioned perfectly once again.

As stated, both of these are fairly unusual examples of Glock pistol stoppages. Nevertheless, after reading the section below on clearing stoppages, you will see that regardless of what causes a failure to feed/fire, the remedy is the same. Also, it is comforting to note that neither failure could be attributed to the Glock pistol involved: one resulted from faulty ammunition, the other from a defective aftermarket installation by an unqualified individual.

Failures to Extract

Extraction failures usually result in a double-feed condition: one round in the chamber with another round pressed hard against it as if also trying to enter the chamber. This situation frequently confounds people; trainers often see shooters fumbling and struggling with a pistol trying to clear a double-feed stoppage.

Here's what a double feed looks like. The second round's nose can be seen jammed hard against the chambered round's base as it's held there by pressure of the recoil and magazine springs.

The reason a double-feed seems difficult to clear is that two of the strongest springs in the pistol are working against one another, combining to resist clearing. The recoil spring is pushing the second round's nose hard into the first (chambered) round's base, while at the same time the magazine spring (through the follower) is pushing the second round (and any below it in the magazine) hard up into the open action.

Many individuals with double-feed-disabled pistols, unable to remove the magazine by tugging on it, attempt to lock the slide open. Actually, this is necessary with virtually all pistols except Glocks. But most people lack the ability to lock the slide open quickly and efficiently under such conditions. So far as Glocks are concerned, however, double-feed stoppages can be cleared rapidly without having to waste time locking the slide open. (See "Tap-Rack-Bang" below for clearing procedures.)

Double-feeds can happen when a cartridge is left chambered while the slide cycles, resulting in another trying to chamber behind it. This can happen when the extractor slips off the chambered cartridge's rim or when the extractor or extractor depressor plunger is damaged, broken, or missing. A double-feed can also occur because a defective magazine released two rounds instead of one.

Failures to Eject

Failures to eject, commonly called "stovepipes," usually result when the slide returns before the ejecting empty casing can clear the ejection port. Because the forward-moving slide begins closing the ejection port early, the casing being ejected is trapped between the breechface and the forward edge of the port. Viewed from the shooter's perspective, a trapped empty casing can look like a tiny smokestack, thus the idiomatic name.

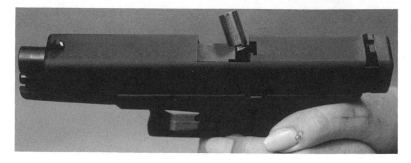

A stovepipe (failure to eject). Here, an empty casing has been trapped, by the closing slide, between the firing chamber at the rear of the barrel and the breechface.

While a damaged ejector can cause stovepipes, more often they result from an early-closing slide trapping the ejecting casing before it can clear the port. Usually, but not always, an early-closing slide is due to incomplete slide cycling. If the slide doesn't get all the way back before it starts forward, the ejecting casing might not have enough time to clear the ejection port.

Under some circumstances, however, overpowered ammunition can accelerate the slide with such force that it bangs against the stops and returns early, trapping the ejecting casing and causing a stovepipe. But, as stated, much more often stovepipes result from just the opposite: a slow-moving slide that fails to make it all the way back before the recoil spring overcomes the rearward force and begins moving the slide forward sooner than it would normally.

Therefore, stovepipes can be caused by anything that interferes with complete slide cycling (i.e., anything that diminishes recoil force or impedes slide movement). Sometimes incomplete slide cycling is due to an excessively dirty pistol, although Glocks perform much better under such conditions than do other pistols. Also, any pistol might stovepipe if the shooter's thumb or finger rubs against the slide.

A common cause of stovepipes in Glock pistols—possibly the most common—is failure to provide sufficient resistance to recoil. If the shooter fails to "back up" the pistol's recoil and allows the entire gun to move back with the force of recoil, even ever so slightly, the recoil spring force will overcome the recoil force and the slide will begin moving forward early, possibly trapping the ejecting casing.

Trainers often see this in shooters who have previously fired only revolvers (thus the term "revolver wrist"), as well as women and improperly trained one-handed shooters. It's very easy to remedy: merely explain the phenomenon and how the wrist must be locked and the forearm muscles stiffened slightly, and the problem usually disappears. (See the "Action Balance" section of Chapter 13 for more on this.)

Tap-Rack-Bang

The classic "tap-rack-bang" drill is the first thing to attempt for most stoppages in tactically exigent situations. It works like this:

1. Tap: forcefully tap the magazine floorplate upward into the magazine well to ensure that it's properly seated.
2. Rack: fully cycle (often called "racking") the action.
3. Bang: fire the pistol.

The tap-rack-bang drill can be accomplished quickly and easily and, as stated, is likely enough to clear the stoppage and return the pistol to working order that it should be tried first in most cases.

Failures to feed are corrected by tap-rack-bang unless the magazine is missing or empty, and in such cases the drill will most likely reveal that one of those conditions exists. The most common cause of failures to feed—improperly seated magazines—is corrected by the "tap" portion of the drill.

Failures to fire are corrected by the tap-rack-bang drill because the offending round will be extracted and ejected during the "rack" portion of the drill, replaced by a fresh one, and fired during the "bang" portion of the drill.

Stovepipes, at least in Glock pistols, are cleared by the tap-rack-bang procedure. The trapped casing will fall away from the gun during the "rack" portion of the drill; also, a fresh round will be chambered during that portion of the procedure. (Merely removing the trapped casing will not return the pistol to operating condition. The slide must have gone all the way back to be able to strip a fresh round from the magazine, and that will not have happened if a stovepipe occurred.)

Double-feeds in just about all pistols require that the slide be locked open, the magazine removed, then the slide worked vigorously through several full cycles so the second double-fed round falls out through the magazine well. The magazine is reinserted, and finally, the slide is unlocked so it can strip a fresh round from the magazine and chamber it. But, as stated, Glocks don't require nearly so much mucking about to get back into working condition following a double-feed stoppage. Merely "rip" the magazine from the well (get it all the way out, but no further than that), immediately reinsert and "tap" it into place, "rack" the slide, and the pistol is ready to go "bang."

• • • • •

Most Glock pistol stoppages—e.g., failures to feed, failures to fire, and stovepipes—can be cleared quickly using the tap-rack-bang procedure; double-feeds require the addition of "rip" before tap-rack-bang.

If it happens that the tap-rack-bang drill doesn't correct the stoppage, whatever does result from the procedure often provides sufficient diagnostic information to enable a properly trained shooter, especially when using a Glock, to clear the stoppage and return the gun to working order quickly enough to be effective.

Reloading

One of the most significant tactical advantages pistols have over revolvers is the ability to be reloaded quickly. Chapter 13 explains why this is true, and here is where the actual reloading procedures are described. The three ways in which pistols are reloaded are: 1) when empty with slide locked open, 2) when empty with slide in battery (closed), and 3) when only partially empty (called tactical reloading).

Empty, Slide Open
Most pistols are designed so that the slide remains open after the last round of ammunition in the gun has

been fired, and that's the most common configuration from which a pistol will be reloaded in a gunfight.

As discussed in Chapter 4, "The CHP and Scottsdale Reports," the California Highway Patrol made a big deal of the fact that Glock magazines tend not to drop free when released. Their concerns, like those of many trainers and others, have their roots in competitive shooting games. The generally accepted pistol reloading technique there is:

1. Grasp a fresh magazine securely with the nongun hand.
2. Release the magazine in the gun and allow it to fall free.
3. Bring the fresh magazine up to the gun and insert it into the magazine well.

Those who believe that Glock magazines' tendency to not drop free from the pistol when released is a liability insist that the standard reloading technique for Glock pistols is too slow and complex. Here's what they're complaining about:

1. Simultaneously grasp the in-gun magazine at the base (using the cutouts provided) with the nongun hand and actuate the magazine catch (release) with the gun hand.
2. Remove the empty magazine and discard it.
3. Grasp a fresh magazine with the nongun hand, bring it up, and insert it into the magazine well.

With a little practice, Glock pistols can be reloaded virtually as quickly as pistols with magazines that drop free when released.

When necessary during reloading, most people drop (release) the slide by actuating the slide release. There's nothing wrong with doing this, but there is a more tactically sound method: holding the pistol in the normal fashion with the gun hand, grasp the slide by reaching over the top (be careful not to cross the muzzle with your hand/arm) with your nongun hand; move the slide to the rear stop (it can move back only a little); then release it and allow the full force of the recoil spring to drive it into battery. A fresh round from the magazine will be chambered in the process.

This method is more tactically sound than fumbling with the slide-release lever. On most pistols, Glocks included, slide releases are such that release, especially under stress, is not facilitated. Using the nongun hand as described above allows for a more positive and faster release and return to service.

Empty, Slide Closed

Sometimes, for whatever reason, the slide fails to lock open after the last round has been fired. Unless you're counting your shots (and you shouldn't be!), you won't know for certain that the pistol is actually empty. You'll have experienced a failure to fire and, therefore, should execute the tap-rack-bang drill. It won't fix the problem, so you should proceed to check for ammunition in the gun.

If you do as many do and crack open the ejection port by moving the slide back slightly to see if there's a round in the chamber, you're wasting precious time. Better to simply perform a standard reloading drill combined with an immediate tap-rack-bang. This will replenish the empty magazine with a loaded one and chamber a round from the fresh magazine immediately thereafter.

Tactical Reloading

Modern high-tech pistols tend to have far greater magazine capacity than do older guns. But merely because there are more rounds in the gun doesn't mean you should forget sound ammunition management techniques. On the contrary, doing so negates one of the chief advantages of these marvelous defense pistols.

Suppose that during a gunfight a break in the action makes it tactically desirable to replenish a partially depleted magazine with a fully loaded one. Regardless of how much ammunition you have available, in a deadly confrontation it is foolish to jettison completely a magazine containing useable ammunition; you should store it where it's retrievable if needed. Thus the tactical reload.

Glock magazines' tendency to not fall free when released is actually a distinct advantage for tactical reloading, which is accomplished as follows:

1. With the nongun hand, grasp a fresh magazine and bring it up to the gun, simultaneously actuating the magazine catch (release).
2. Place the fresh magazine between the middle and ring fingers (or, alternatively, between the ring and little fingers) of the gun hand. The magazine should be placed there with the top toward the pistol (bullets facing forward, the same direction the muzzle is facing) and the base away.
3. With the nongun hand, remove the empty magazine from the well and store it where it can be retrieved if needed.
4. Still with the nongun hand, retrieve the fresh magazine from the gun hand's fingers and insert it into the magazine well. Seat it with conviction.

NOTE: It is not necessary to perform tap-rack-bang in conjunction with or following a tactical reload because there will be a round of ammunition in the chamber. Remember, you opted to remove a partially depleted magazine from a fully functioning, ready-to-fire pistol for tactical reasons. Merely swapping one magazine for another changes nothing vis-a-vis the chamber or the round that was in it before the tactical reload was performed.

Low-Light Techniques

Because about 70 percent of confrontations involving guns occur in low light, it's important that we understand as much as possible about how we and our firearms function in that environment.

For most of us, dim-light adaptation to a point that will allow us to use a firearm acceptably in a tactically exigent situation takes from two to twenty minutes. For many things that's not too bad, but if a deadly confrontation begins just as we're first encountering a poorly lit environment, we're in big trouble. Remember, the average time for an armed encounter is only 3.2 seconds, so even if we're among those who adapt way down in the two-minute range, it'll all be over by then.

Although not all confrontations occur just as a person enters a dim-light situation, the bad guys often know how to maximize their advantages (which translates to minimizing ours) and will catch us at a disadvantage whenever possible. So even if we've adapted to a poor light environment as much as we're going to, it's important that our firearm gives us as much of an edge as possible. Glocks do that.

One handy little feature is the ejector. When the chamber is empty, the ejector is flush to the slide (on the right side). But when there's a round in the chamber, the ejector's leading edge projects slightly. In other words, if you move your trigger finger (assuming a right-handed shooter) up to the ejection port and feel the leading edge of the ejector (located at the trailing edge of the ejection port), flush indicates an empty chamber and slightly projecting indicates a loaded chamber. Not a real big deal, but during a tactically exigent situation it is a little one-handed, silent reassurance that the pistol is ready for action, eliminating the need for two-handed, light-assisted, noise-inducing visual verification.

A huge disadvantage of using a conventionally sight-ed pistol in dim light is that the all-important front sight "washes-out" against the target. Even in conditions just slightly darker than normal daylight, the front sight frequently blends in with the target so much that it virtually disappears. Glock pistols provide some advantage over others in this regard.

Glocks' natural pointing ability means that when we first bring our pistol up and into action in dim-light (or even dark) conditions, it's more likely than other pistols to be properly aligned. That's important because with so little time, we can't afford to throw away even the least little bit doing such things as making minor adjustments in pistol/hand/arm alignment.

Glock night sights—available as factory options or aftermarket installations—afford significant tactical advantages over conventional nonilluminated sights.

Self-luminous night sights are tiny canisters of encapsulated radioactive tritium that enable the shooter to use visual reference cues even when conventional sights would be completely lost in darkness. (See Chapter 10, "Glock Pistols from the Inside Out," for more about night sights.) Most night sights on handguns, including both Armson Trijicon and Meprolites, are of the three-dot variety: two dots on either side of the rear sight notch and a third on the front sight.

Meprolight night sights (left), Trijicon night sights (center), and standard Glock factory fixed sights (right).

Such sights are aligned when all three dots are lined up on a single horizontal plane, as viewed by the shooter. When the gun is brought up onto target during daylight conditions, many peripheral visual cues are available that disappear in darkness. As a result, someone raising a gun toward a target for the first time in poorly lit conditions is often shocked to discover how much more difficult it is in the absence of the visual cues one hardly notices in daylight.

While three-dot sights pose no particular problem in daylight, initial and subsequent sight acquisition is significantly more difficult in low light or darkness. Some have even expressed concern that the three-dot night sights could be aligned in darkness with the front dot outside one of the others without the shooter being aware of his or her mistake. Perhaps anything is possible, but it seems rather unlikely that anyone reasonably familiar with handguns could err so grossly. Regardless, Glocks' natural pointing tendencies make such misalignment highly unlikely.

Other Tactical Exigencies

Because of their many "user-friendly" attributes (to borrow a term from the computer industry), Glock pistols are generally tactically superior, something even more pronounced in most tactically demanding situations.

Using Glock Pistols One-Handed

Sometimes it is necessary or desirable to use a defense pistol with only one hand, such as when your usual gun hand or arm is injured. Even though it's best to use both hands on a gun in tactical situations, there are times when only one is available even when there's been no injury. Your nongun hand may be otherwise occupied, for example, maintaining balance on a staircase or around a corner or edge of a barricade, or assisting or controlling another person, such as a child, elderly person, or someone who is injured or hysterical.

Glock pistols are particularly well-suited to one-hand operations. They are devoid of external safeties, decocking levers, and flip-flaps of the sort found on most modern pistols. In fact, they have only two external devices requiring affirmative actuation: a magazine catch (release) and a slide-stop lever.

The magazine catch is designed to be operated with only one hand, so it's not a problem for a shooter so restricted. When using your left hand (regardless of whether or not you are left-handed), merely actuate the release with the trigger finger instead of the thumb, as would be the case when holding the pistol in the right hand.

The slide-stop lever can be operated with the index finger when the pistol is held left-handed, but for some this is difficult. An alternative for one-handed manual slide actuation is to utilize some hard-surfaced, more or less square-edged object such as a tabletop, chair back or arm, or the side of a slightly open drawer. Many pistols do not lend themselves well to this technique, but Glocks, with their massive "squared" slides, are well-suited to it. Here's how it works:

Holding the pistol in the usual one-handed manner, place the muzzle end against the corner or edge of a suitable object so that the front or upper corner of the slide is against the object but the end of the barrel is not. CAVEAT: Be careful to position the pistol carefully so that only the front of the slide—and not the muzzle itself or the front sight—presses against the object. Once situated, push the pistol forward so that the slide (the front end of which is pressing against the object) moves to the rear.

This technique can be used for various things, e.g., to lock the slide open, cycle the slide to chamber a round, or release an already locked-open slide. To accomplish the latter, position the pistol against a suitable object, as described above, and push the slide back against the stops. Then quickly pull the pistol away from the object it's pressing against, allowing the slide to snap into battery with the full force of the recoil spring. CAVEAT: when using the left hand, be certain that your index finger doesn't interfere with free movement of the slide-stop lever, or the slide may not release.

For the reasons stated above, Glock pistols are easier than most to fire one-handed. This is even more true during extra-high-stress situations, such as when one is injured or otherwise required to do extraordinary things such as firing one-handed.

When firing a Glock one-handed, it helps to cock the pistol about 15 degrees to the right (clockwise). This allows gravity to assist the normal ejection process just a bit and might avoid what could have been a failure to eject otherwise.

It must be remembered that Glock pistols demand a firm platform from which to operate. Even more than when firing with two hands, it's important to keep your gun-hand wrist locked and your forearm straight and tight to avoid stovepipes. If a stovepipe should occur, merely combine the appropriate techniques described above to clear it:

1. Holding the pistol in the usual one-handed manner, "tap" the floorplate of the in-place magazine against a hard surface such as a tabletop, a chair, the ground, etc.
2. Place the muzzle end of the slide against a suitable object as described above.
3. "Rack" the slide by pushing the pistol forward to the stops against the object. This will release the trapped (stovepiped) casing and allow it to fall free.
4. Quickly remove the pistol from the object, allowing the slide to snap into battery with the full force of the recoil spring. This will chamber a fresh round, rendering the pistol ready to go "bang."

Multiple and/or Moving Targets

Because Glock pistols cycle so rapidly and have triggers that can be reset so quickly, they are ideally suited to deal with the ever-increasing threat of multiple targets.

Because of their natural pointing tendency, low felt recoil, and other "user-friendly" features, Glock pistols also facilitate success when dealing with moving targets.

• • • • • •

The scope and magnitude of Glock pistols' various operations-oriented advantages are remarkable in themselves, and when coupled with the design-oriented advantages described in the previous chapter, they add up to a truly awe-inspiring weapon. All in all, the twenty-first century technology of which Glock is justly so proud makes Glock pistols a clear first choice among modern, high-tech defense pistols.

CHAPTER 15

Accessories and Special Stuff

his chapter covers factory-manufactured options, accessories, a few little-known and/or rarely seen items available for Glock pistols, Glock-manufactured non-firearm-related items, and aftermarket items available for Glock pistols.

Glock-Manufactured Options and Little-Known and/or Rarely Seen Items

There are only a few factory-manufactured options and extras for Glock pistols, and most are items almost no one is aware of and/or has never even seen a photograph of.

+2 Magazines

As mentioned in previous chapters, Glock produces "+2" magazines for the Models 17 and 19 pistols. These differ from the regular magazines only in that the floorplate is different. The +2 floorplate, instead of being flat, is triangular-shaped when viewed in profile. The forward face extends downward about 3/4 inch lower than that of the regular floorplate; thus, the bottom of the +2 floorplate slopes upward toward the rear, giving the accessory a triangular profile. The +2 magazines are available commercially as complete units, although certified Glock armorers can purchase the +2 floorplates from the factory.

As of this writing, Glock produced +2 magazines only for its 9mm pistols. As the .40 S&W, 10mm, and .45 ACP magazines have a different floorplate design (see Chapter 13, "Design Features"), it is uncertain just when, or even if, the factory will produce +2 magazines for those calibers. However, +2 floorplates for 9mm magazines will fit on .40-caliber magazine tubes. Even though the .40-caliber magazine has a subfloorplate with a retaining post that fits into a corresponding hole in the actual floorplate, the .40-caliber magazines seem to function satisfactorily with the subfloorplate removed and a 9mm +2 floorplate replacing the standard .40-caliber one. It should be noted that the factory does not endorse this. (See the section below on aftermarket items for more information about +2 magazine floorplates.)

Extended Magazine Catch

Glock makes an extended magazine catch for the small (Models 19 and 23) and midsize (Models 17, 17L, 18, and 22) receivers. It is standard on the Model 17L and optional on the others.

The extended magazine catch is 3/32 inch longer than the standard magazine catch. That's considerably more in this application than it seems; an extended catch is quite different from a regular one when installed on a pistol.

The extended magazine catch projects 3/32 inch further out from the grip of Models 17, 17L (shown here), 18, 19, 22, and 23 than does the standard-length magazine catch.

As of this writing, Glock installed its extended magazine catch (originally made for the smaller-frame guns) as the standard in the large-receiver pistols (Models 20 and 21). There was no extended catch available for the Models 20 and 21. This did not conform to the factory parts list, however, which showed the standard magazine catch for the Models 20 and 21 as a different, discrete part number. In regard to this, the factory claimed that it eventually would have an extended magazine catch available for the large-frame guns. This will undoubtedly benefit competition shooters, many of whom eagerly awaited the Model 21's introduction (which finally occurred in late spring of 1991).

Lanyard

The lanyard hole at the very bottom of the backstrap is only about 3/32 inch in diameter.

Ever wonder what the little hole at the bottom of the backstrap is for? At least one person I know clips a key ring into it from which to hang his pistol when using public rest rooms, thus solving a dilemma long pondered by disciples of Jeff Cooper. Such use is not, however, what Gaston Glock had in mind when he designed that little hole in his gun.

It is there to accommodate a device known as Glock part #1764, lanyard. This is a nylonlike, looped cord in more or less standard lanyard fashion, with a metal clip (not unlike my friend uses in public rest rooms, by the way) on one end designed to go through the hole at the bottom of the backstrap. Lanyards, which were originally intended to prevent cavalry officers from losing their revolvers (the lanyard connected the gun to the officer's epaulet, saddle, or some other part of the man or his horse), are seldom seen on pistols anymore, especially in America, although one police department (in Michigan) did order them for its Model 17s.

Extended Magazine

Originally developed for the select-fire Model 18, the 33-round extended magazine will fit and function in any of Glock's 9mm pistols. It is identical to the Models 17 and 19 +2 magazines, except for being considerably longer.

The factory extended magazine, shown here with 33 rounds of 9mm Parabellum ammunition.

Glock has a firm policy of selling the extended magazine only to law enforcement agencies and departments.

Training Magazine

Many trainers, departments, and agencies have policies that prohibit using duty magazines for training. The thought is that magazines frequently abused during various training exercises may have diminished reliability and, therefore, may be undesirable for duty use.

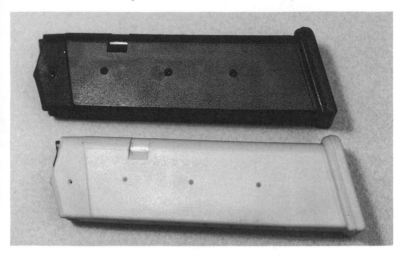

Glock's orange training magazine (bottom) next to a standard black duty magazine (top), right side of both shown.

This is not a new notion, nor is it especially remarkable. For years, folks have identified certain magazines to be used only for training and have marked them in various ways. Not long after the California Highway Patrol placed its order for seven thousand S&W Model 4006 pistols, Smith & Wesson President Steve Melvin told me that CHP also purchased a large quantity of magazines with various colored floorplates (the floorplates on Model 4006 magazines are synthetic and are easily manufactured in colors), presumably to be used for transition and training purposes.

Just as Smith & Wesson's synthetic magazine floorplates lend themselves easily to being color-impregnated, so do Glock's polymer ones. Little known to civilians, Glock produces a bright orange magazine, sold only to law enforcement agencies and departments. Differing only in the color of the polymer, Glock's orange training magazines simply provide an option to instructors who prefer to keep training magazines separate and easily distinguishable from their duty magazines.

The orange training magazine (bottom) and the standard black duty magazine (top). In the center is a standard magazine to which Threat Management Institute had the aftermarket process known as Z-Coat applied in pea-green.

Training Pistol

If polymer magazines can be made in a color other than black, why not an entire polymer receiver? Why not indeed!

In fact, Glock makes a little-known receiver in bright red! That's right—fire-engine red. Visually, Glock's red receiver is identical to the black ones in every respect except color. Despite the fact that their largest component is red—these things are commonly referred to as "red guns"—they actually have substantial amounts of black on them, made all the more noticeable by the stark contrast.

A Model 17 training pistol. Only the receiver is red polymer; everything else is black as in the standard production pistol.

Looking at a "red" Glock Model 17, one actually sees an all-black slide assembly, plus black slide-lock ends, trigger, slide-lock lever, magazine catch, trigger and trigger housing pins, and (if in place) the floorplate and that portion of the magazine tube normally visible.

What is the purpose of a red Glock, and why red instead of orange like the training magazines? The purpose of a red Glock is, like that of the orange training magazines, to distinguish it from a normal duty pistol. But the similarity ends there, which is why the pistol is red, not orange. The orange training magazine is fully functional; it's just colored differently for differentiation purposes. The red Glocks, however, are not functional; in fact, they're permanently deactivated.

Both the orange magazine and red pistol are colored so as to be readily identifiable as training devices not for duty use. The magazine is orange, signifying that it's fully functional; the pistol is red, signifying that it has been deactivated. If the orange training magazine were used inadvertently in a duty weapon, it would most likely work just fine. But if a red pistol were inadvertently used for duty/defense, the results would be disastrous.

There are certain things trainers do during firearms and tactical instruction that are impossible or difficult to accomplish without violating fundamental gun safety rules. Some schools of thought hold that doing such things with a working duty gun, or something that looks just like one, sends the wrong message to students: that operational safety rules needn't always be adhered to. For those who subscribe to that philosophy, using a deactivated gun that is clearly identified as such for those things that violate fundamental gun safety rules but nevertheless must be done during training avoids sending a wrong message to students.

Another school of thought holds that fundamental gun safety rules should never be broken. This applies especially to the rule that mandates adhering to a single standard of behavior: one that would be appropriate for a loaded, ready-to-fire gun regardless of whether or not the gun in one's hand was loaded and ready to fire or, indeed, incapable of firing for any reason. For subscribers to this tenet, trainers and other people should always behave as if their guns were loaded, even if it is a deactivated one clearly identified as such by its bright red color.

Arguments of doctrine aside, Glock's red guns are deactivated permanently and irrevocably by welding shut the opening in the breechface from which the firing pin normally emerges to strike and detonate a chambered round of ammunition. There is a problem, however, of a potentially serious nature: the deactivation is accomplished entirely within the components of the slide; the red receiver is exactly the same as a black one, and just as functional. This means that a normal slide can easily be fitted to a red receiver to make a fully functional pistol and, conversely, the deactivated slide assembly can easily be installed on a black receiver, resulting in a nonworking pistol that can't be identified as such.

Cutaway Pistol

Another little-known and rarely seen pistol Glock produces is the "cutaway." Obviously training devices, Glock's cutaway pistols are just what their name implies: standard production models with various openings cut into them at strategic locations so the inner workings can be studied.

A cutaway Model 19 with orange plastic training ammunition cartridges installed to further enhance visualization.

Most of the openings are in the cutaway pistol's left side—nine, compared to two on the right side. That's because there's more interesting stuff to see on the left side, but it shouldn't be understood to mean that what is on the right side isn't just as important to learn about.

One of the two openings on the right side is very extensive and actually includes cuts on the slide and receiver that are mated to form one large opening. The slide cut runs the length of the ejection port and extends up from the bottom edge about 1/4 inch. The receiver cut runs along the top of the frame, roughly the width of the grip and extends down about 1/4 inch.

This large cut exposes a lot of inner components and shows their relationship to one another. At the front edge of the opening one can see the end of the recoil spring and recoil-spring tube, the slide lock, the locking block, both barrel lugs and a portion of the firing chamber, the bottom of the firing-pin safety, and just about all of the trigger bar. When the trigger is actuated, the upward-projecting trigger-bar tab can be seen releasing the firing-pin safety.

Through the smaller opening on the cutaway pistol's right side can be seen the rearward-projecting tab of the trigger bar and the upper portion of the connector, including the angled ramp. When the trigger is actuated, the rearward-projecting tab of the trigger bar can be seen contacting the connector's angled ramp. Upon further pressing of the trigger, the trigger bar can be seen as it's forced down along the angled ramp. Very close inspection, possibly with the aid of a light, will reveal a glimpse of the rear portion of the cruciform sear plate (an integral part of the trigger bar) and the downward-projecting tab of the firing pin. A better view of these components and their mutual relationship is available through a corresponding opening at the rear of the slide's left side.

It's difficult to say which of the cutaway pistol's nine left-side openings affords the most interesting view, but the small one at the rear of the slide is certainly among those vying for top contender. What is significant there is the aft end of the cruciform sear plate and the downward-projecting tab of the firing pin. It's very informative to study their relationship and to see what happens when the trigger bar is forced down the connector's angled ramp sufficiently to finally release the firing pin.

Just below and a bit forward of that opening is another small one. This one reveals the trigger spring (original coil-type or New York) and its installation and attachment to the trigger housing mechanism and downward projecting tab of the cruciform sear plate's longitudinal portion.

Another extremely interesting opening is in the slide. Along a portion of the left side and top, it clearly displays the firing-pin assembly and the firing-pin safety. Repeated partial trigger actuation (just to the point where resistance is felt as the trigger bar contacts the connector's angled ramp) shows how all these parts work.

There are other openings that reveal the inside of the barrel and firing chamber, the extractor, the trigger safety, and the magazine—which has corresponding openings so its innards can also be examined.

Glock's cutaway training pistol is a marvelous way to learn the inner workings of a fantastic firearm.

Amphibious Firing-Pin Spring Cups

Among the least-known and most rarely seen options Glock offers, these are often referred to as underwater spring cups. Spring cups (#8 on the exploded parts diagram) are essentially two halves of a split bushing used to assist the firing pin and to retain its spring.

A pair of amphibious spring cups (middle pair) compared to standard spring cups (outer pair), shown with fine-point writing pen for size comparison.

Amphibious firing-pin spring cups are just like regular spring cups except for one important difference: there are four relatively wide flutes in the cups' larger collar. As a result, when installed, the underwater spring cups appear to have four lugs separated by four wide longitudinal cuts, or channels, where the larger collar normally is.

The purpose of the channels is to allow water to pass back and forth past the cups to avoid the formation of a hydraulic lock in the area of the firing-pin spring. Such a lock could result in disaster in more ways than one.

But just as Glock's amphibious firing-pin spring cups avoid disaster as described above, they can cause it in other ways, principally by severely damaging the eardrums of a person whose unprotected ears are beneath the surface in the vicinity of a Glock that is fired underwater. To Glock, this is a problem of such significant proportions that no amphibious firing-pin spring cups will be sold to any customer other than special units of the military. And even then, an authorized representative of the unit must sign a waiver and letter of understanding, the contents of which are reproduced in their entirety here:

GLOCK, INC.
P.O. Box 369
Smyrna, Georgia 30081 U.S.A.
Telephone: (404) 432-1202
Telex: 543353 Glock Atl UD
Fax: (404) 433-8719

WAIVER/LETTER OF UNDERSTANDING

Re: Glock Amphibious Firing Pin Spring Cups

Within the limitations given below and in the attached Product Information, the Glock Model-17/19 9x19 mm can be fired on semi-automatic mode underwater.

Note: • The amphibious firing pin spring cups for the Glock Models 17/19 are an optional piece of equipment, not incorporated as standard.

Accessories and Special Stuff

- Tests have been performed in depths up to 28 inches below the water surface. There are no records so far concerning safety aspects in depths exceeding these limits.

- The use of amphibious firing pin spring cups are strictly limited for Glock Model-17 pistols with serial numbers (barrel) starting from AN000 for safety reasons.

- The tests concerning effects to the human body by the shock and sound waves that occur when firing under water are still ongoing and sufficient results have not been obtained yet. Damage to the human ear may occur so proper ear protection must be worn when firing Glock pistols underwater.

- Only standard commercial FMJ 9mm Parabellum ammunition shall be used (no high velocity or super loads).

The Manufacturer, only and exclusively, warrants for the proper function, within the given criteria, of underwater firing. Before release of the product for underwater firing, only demonstrations and tests may be made, firing with the gun submerged in water.

Factory tests were made in a pool with the gun about 1.5 feet below the surface. Before firing make absolutely certain that:

- the barrel of the gun points toward a direction that is free of persons or obstructions, and

- no persons except the demonstrator are inside the pool, and

- the demonstrator keeps his unprotected ears and nose well clear from the surface, outside the water.

It is strongly recommended to have this demonstration performed solely by factory personnel or experienced armorers trained by the factory.

GLOCK, INC.

Karl Walter
Vice President

KFW:ada

I have read the foregoing and understand that proper ear protection must be worn when firing Glock pistols underwater. I have also read and agree to adhere to all other safety recommendations as outlined in the foregoing text.

Name	Signature
Title	Date

Glock-Manufactured Accessories

Holsters

Glock produces four different holsters made specially for its pistols: a Sport/Combat model, a Police model, a Sport/Duty model, and a GI-Type model. All are made out of specially formulated polymer that is soft and pliable, yet surprisingly durable.

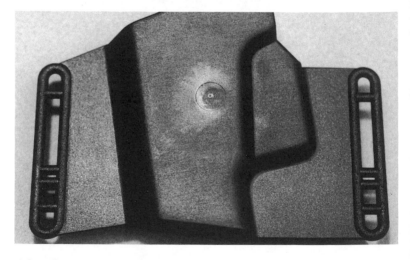

A Sport/Combat holster shown from the left side. Note the four removable posts on each side, used to accommodate holster to various belt thicknesses.

The *Sport/Combat model* is a belt-slide-type holster that covers the pistol from about an inch forward of the trigger guard to back just enough to cover the magazine catch. It is totally ambidextrous, so it works for strong-side and cross-draw positions on the belts of both right- and left-handers. Not surprisingly for a Glock-designed product, it is very ingenious.

A Sport/Combat holster with a Model 23 pistol installed. This is one of the most comfortable ways in which to wear a Glock pistol.

The Sport/Combat holster has a retention device despite the fact that it fits quite snugly. It is difficult to extricate a pistol from one of these holsters. As someone who has worn a Glock Sport/Combat holster all day, every day, for several years, I can attest to the fact that it is virtually impossible for the pistol to be accidentally dislodged. In fact, it requires a special technique just to unholster the pistol smoothly, without struggling with it. The trick is to snatch the pistol directly upward to break it free from the retaining device situated near the trigger guard.

Glock's Sport/Combat holster has no thumb break or other retaining strap. Intended for plainclothes and/or sport usage, there is no need for such retention capability, which is, after all, designed to defeat weapon-grab attempts.

The Sport/Combat holster is equipped with dual belt slots that can be permanently sized to accommodate belts of 1 1/8, 1 1/4, 1 5/8, 2 1/8, or 2 1/2 inches in width. Each 2 1/2-inch slot on the ends of the holster has four integral dividers that can be removed (by cutting) to accommodate belts of the above-listed widths. Also, for some of the widths less than 2 1/2 inches, the height at which the holster will ride on one's belt can be adjusted slightly.

This little holster weighs only about 1 1/2 ounces and is extremely comfortable to wear under clothing such as a coat, jacket, or shirt worn outside one's pants or skirt. And in nonconcealment situations where weapon retention against take-away attempts is not an issue (such as in a training or sport environment), this holster is an excellent choice.

The *Police model* is a fully enclosed police-type holster complete with thumb-break strap. When holstered, the pistol's trigger guard and magazine catch are fully covered. In fact, when holstered with the thumb-break strap snapped, only the front strap below the trigger guard, the back strap from the recurve down, and that portion of the grip between them are exposed.

The Police holster is swivel-mounted on a flat polymer plate equipped with two slots to accommodate standard duty belt sizes of 1 3/4 and 2 1/2 inches. The holster hangs down a few inches and swivels so as to be comfortable for the carrier while seated in a vehicle, and it can be removed from the belt plate without the belt itself having to be removed or unbuckled. It weighs less than 4 ounces.

The Police holster has three holes—two 3/16-inch and one 3/32-inch—in the bottom (when the holster is in the normal on-belt orientation) to avoid moisture buildup or water collection.

The *Sport/Duty holster* is identical to the Police holster except that instead of having the drop plate and swivel, it is equipped with an integral slot to accommodate belt widths up to 1 3/4 inches. It weighs only 2 1/2 ounces.

A Sport/Duty holster shown from the right side.

The *GI-Type holster* is similar to the Police model except that it is designed to be worn on a standard military web belt.

Magazine Pouch

The Glock magazine pouch is the functional equivalent of the Glock Sport/Combat holster. It is equipped with the identical belt slots that can be permanently adjusted for belt widths as described above for the Sport/Combat holster.

A Sport/Duty holster from the left side. Note the integrally molded thumb break strap.

While the pouch itself is ambidextrous, magazines will only fit into it one way. Therefore, tactically diligent individuals must take care to install the pouches on their belts with the longer edge facing the front and the shorter edge to the rear. This ensures that the bullets of the loaded rounds will face forward, thus being oriented correctly in the hand when grasped, removed, and brought up to the gun for insertion into the magazine well.

The magazine pouches have an integral detent inside the cavity that mates with the catch recess on the magazine. This provides more than sufficient retention and eliminates any need for retaining straps, snaps, or flaps.

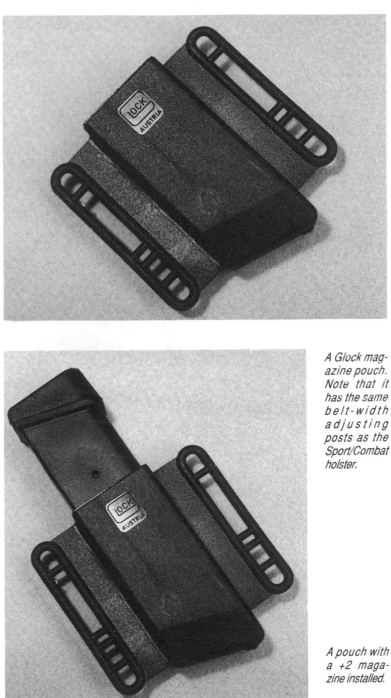

A Glock magazine pouch. Note that it has the same belt-width adjusting posts as the Sport/Combat holster.

A pouch with a +2 magazine installed.

Like the above-described Glock holsters, the magazine pouch is extremely light. It weighs a mere 3/4 ounce. And like the Police holster, it has a drain hole on the bottom.

Magazine Loader

Familiar to anyone who owns or has used a Glock pistol, these handy items not only come with every gun Glock sells, they're available separately. They facilitate magazine loading immensely; once you're accustomed to using them, you can load a magazine quickly without devoting much energy or attention to the task.

A Model 17 with a +2 floorplate installed, shown with a loader and the 19 rounds of 9mm Parabellum ammunition it will hold. The loader greatly facilitates loading, saving fingertips in the process.

Standard Austrian Military Web Belt

This belt is made from durable industrial-grade nylon with standard metal grommets, three-high, spaced about every 1 3/8 inches. It is Austria's version of olive drab (OD), which is slightly more grayish than the American military version.

A Glock military-style web belt.

There are two plastic retaining devices for that portion of each end of the belt that loops through the buckle to adjust for waist size. The buckle itself, an OD-colored unit made of high-impact-resistant polymer, is Glock-designed and features a unique twist-and-pull release. Glock claims the release is "simple," but at first it takes a little getting used to. The buckle's face is emblazoned with the Austrian eagle.

Glock-Manufactured Nonfirearm-Related Products

Glock produces three noteworthy nonfirearm-related items: the Glock Entrenching Tool and the Glock 78 and Glock 81 field knives.

Entrenching Tool
Sometimes called the "field spade," the Glock Entrenching Tool is a remarkable item. Folded into a 10-by-6-inch package that is only 2 inches thick, it is easily stored or carried using the 1 1/2-inch-thick shaft of the

telescoped (collapsed) handle as a hand grip. It weighs only 24 ounces.

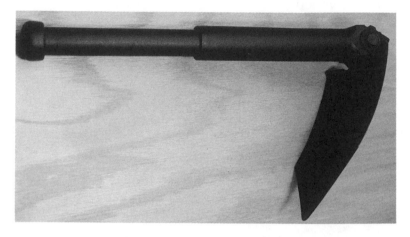

Glock's entrenching tool with blade held open and one of its two handle sections extended.

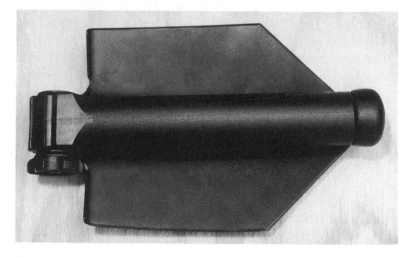

Entrenching tool folded, front side.

The Entrenching Tool uses polymer similar to that used in Glock pistols for its two-section telescoping handle, the base of the saw blade, the handle end cap/saw blade retainer, and the position adjustment knob.

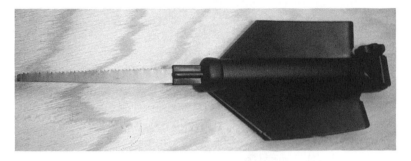

Entrenching tool folded with saw blade in cutting position.

Saw blade and retaining ring/handle end cap near folded entrenching tool; saw blade stores inside handle.

The five-sided, shovel-type blade is made from a single piece of hardened steel, with no rivets or welds to weaken it, and it is surface-treated to prevent corrosion.

The blade is quite rigid, with the two leading edges and the rounded point slightly sharpened. One of Glock's promotional photos shows the blade being used to chop down a small tree using the point and sharpened edges.

The saw blade with screwdriver tip is also made of specially hardened steel. It stores inside the smaller section of the hollow polymer handle, mounts by reversing at the handle's end, and is secured by the same threaded device that retains it—all very neat and clever.

The tool can be used in three modes: 1) folded carry mode, 2) short extension mode (only one handle section extended; Glock calls this "under cover" mode), and 3) fully extended mode. The saw blade can be used in modes 2 and 3. The tool is 10 inches long when folded, 17 1/2 inches long in short extension mode, and 25 inches long when fully extended.

Glock Field Knives

The original Glock Model 78 field knife was developed in close cooperation with the Austrian army's Rangers—its special forces. In addition, various antiterrorist units around the world use the Glock 78 as a multipurpose field knife.

Designed for close-combat situations, the Glock 78 is also balanced for throwing and can be adapted as a bayonet using a special adapter and mount. It features a specially hardened steel alloy blade (surface hardness is 50-55 Rockwell Cone) treated with a nonreflective black anticorrosive coating. The steel thumb rest has an integral bottle opener.

The comfortable handle is made from the now-familiar Glock polymer, as is the unique sheath. The sheath is a single polymer unit, with no screws, rivets, pins, or seams. It features a clever retaining clip that permits one-handed rapid deployment of the knife and an even more clever belt-loop device that allows the sheath to be attached to and removed from a belt up to 2 1/2 inches wide without having to undo the belt.

The Glock Model 81 is identical to the Model 78 except for the addition of a 3 3/4-inch saw segment along the top of the blade.

Glock Model 78 (top) and 81 (bottom) field knives in sheaths.

Models 78 and 81 unsheathed.

Both knives and sheaths are available in black or OD (Austrian version) polymer. In either case, however, the blades are black, having been coated with a special anti-corrosive substance.

A closer look at the thumb guard of a Glock field knife.

A Model 81 field knife sawing through a plank.

Glock Models 78 and 81 have an overall length of 11 1/3 inches, with a blade length of 6 1/2 inches. The knives themselves weigh 7.1 ounces, the sheaths 1.6 ounces, bringing the entire package to a total of only 8.7 ounces.

• • • • •

The entrenching tool and field knives are unique and useful items, even for those of us not in the military. My partner uses a Model 81 in her garden and praises it highly. I carry an entrenching tool and a Model 81 in my car; together they add less than 33 ounces and take up very little room, and even for nonemergencies they come in mighty handy.

Aftermarket Items for Glock Pistols

At first there were no aftermarket products specifically for Glock pistols. Then came a few holsters, followed by an eclectic sprinkling of other items. Here are some examples of what's available:

Magazines
There is a company, U.S.A. Magazines (Clips), that produces aftermarket magazines for Glock pistols. It's been around for a while, making both "regular" and extended-capacity magazines for a variety of rifles and shotguns, but only recently announced several models for Glock pistols.

U.S.A. Magazines (Clips) offers 16-round magazines for the 9mm Models 17 and 19 pistols and 15-round magazines in .40 S&W for Models 22 and 23. All are available in blue or stainless steel, and all have a synthetic follower.

Due to the Glock factory policy prohibiting the sale of the extended magazines to civilians, U.S.A.'s aftermarket extended magazines have generated considerable interest since the announcement of their planned 1990 introduction. U.S.A.'s current catalog offers 30-round magazines in 9mm for the Models 17 and 19,

10mm for the Model 20, and .40 S&W for the Models 22 and 23.

As of this writing, production versions of the 30-round magazines had yet to be shipped, despite numerous indications that they were to be available by then.

Carlos Santizo at U.S.A. was kind enough to send me a prototype 30-round 9mm magazine for examination, evaluation, and testing. I and my associates tested it extensively in Models 17, 19, and 17L pistols during training classes wherein numerous rounds were fired in short periods of time.

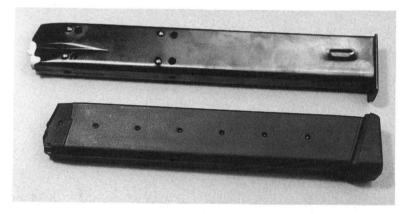

U.S.A. Magazines' 9mm extended magazine for Glock pistols (top) compared to the Glock factory's (bottom).

The prototype 9mm magazine we tested is blue steel with a yellow plastic follower and really doesn't resemble the Glock factory-made 33-round extended magazine. For example, the Glock polymer extended magazine tube (body) is about 1/16 inch wider than the U.S.A.'s blue steel body. On the other hand, the U.S.A.'s body is an inch longer when neither has floorplates installed. The aftermarket magazine uses a flat steel floorplate, while the factory one uses a +2 floorplate. With floorplates installed, the U.S.A. magazine is still 7/8 inch longer, despite the fact that it holds three fewer rounds.

During testing, the U.S.A. magazine's spring seemed to compress in a strange way—it bunched up and snaked around itself inside the tube. The Glock factory spring is made of slightly heavier material, and the U.S.A. spring is significantly longer, containing twenty-eight coils compared to Glock's 17. Also, when each was removed from its tube, the U.S.A.'s spring was decidedly twisted, whereas the Glock's was not.

U.S. A. Magazines' lip and follower designs (left) are very different from Glock's (right).

There are other differences as well: the Glock follower is standard factory issue for 9mm magazines; U.S.A.'s is a unique proprietary design. Also, the Glock magazine has the familiar series of viewing holes down the back side, numbered from 4 to 31, whereas the U.S.A. magazine has but a single large hole in the back with a large "30" stamped beneath it.

Finally, the U.S.A. magazine has several large bumps

in various locations on its body: two on the back side and four on each side. It's unknown what these are for, but during testing the steel magazine fit quite loosely. In fact, it could be moved around a great deal, and sometimes when it was installed and seated in a gun with an open slide, it prevented the slide from closing unless and until it was jiggled about. Occasionally, a pistol using the U.S.A. magazine would not feed a round properly, but when the magazine was jiggled, the round chambered and the slide went into battery without doing more. I am advised that these problems will be remedied on production versions.

+2 Magazine Floorplates

A pair of CATCo +2 aftermarket 9mm floorplates, shown with two 9mm Winchester 147-grain subsonic JHPs.

Accessories and Special Stuff

CATCo, a Reno, Nevada-based company that produces
and sells various firearms-related products, offers a +2
floorplate for Glock Models 17 and 19 magazines. It
appears to be the same as Glock factory +2 floorplates
dimensionally, but there's a large "+2" logo molded into
the bottom surface. A representative told me CATCo
attempted to come as close to Glock's polymer formulation
as possible for its aftermarket +2 magazine floorplates.

While the floorplates were originally designed and
intended for use on 9mm magazines, CATCo claims
they will work porfectly well on Glock's .40-caliber
ones as well. They do fit, but the subfloorplate must
first be removed, and the capacity increases by only one
round instead of two. But considering the fact that as of
this writing Glock had yet to produce a +2 floorplate for
anything other than 9mm magazines, CATCo's addition
of one round gives a .40-caliber user at least a little
extra capacity.

CATCo sells the +2 floorplates and its other products
via a 24-hour telephone order line in Northern California.

Competition-Type Modifications

In Miami, Florida, José Fernandez makes aftermarket
products to modify Glock pistols for competitors. He also
does other in-house modifications.

He makes some steel parts to replace Glock's plastic
ones, such as front sights and guide rods. The front sights
are merely conventionally shaped steel versions of
Glock's plastic ones, the idea being that steel front sights
withstand more abuse than do plastic ones, which can be
a plus for competitors.

Fernandez' steel guide rods are the same as Glock's
factory-supplied plastic ones dimensionally, but there's a
big difference in weight. Available for Models 17, 17L,
19, 20, 22 and 23, these components weigh between 1
and 1 1/2 ounces; that weight is applied forward of the

trigger and is supposed to improve balance and muzzle rise tendency for competitors.

Fernandez' competition compensator installed on a Model 17.

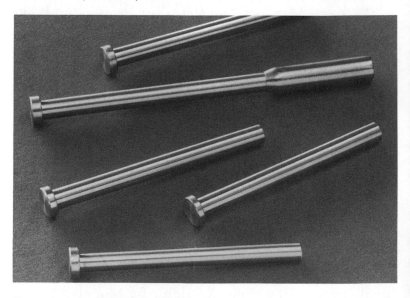

Fernandez' two-piece steel guide rods, designed as aftermarket replacements for Models 20, 22, and 23 polymer recoil spring tubes.

For those interested in more extensive modifications, Fernandez offers such things as Wichita rear sights, his own "Big Mouth" compensator, ported barrels (longitudinal ovals and round holes), rubberized grips, weights for magazines and magazine wells, and beavertail safeties.

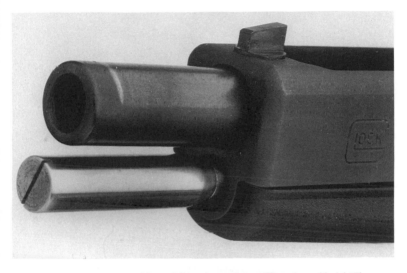

Fernandez' replacement steel front sight and two-piece guide rod on a Model 17L.

• • • • •

Contrary to popular belief, there are actually quite a few factory-manufactured options, accessories, and after-market items available for Glock pistols, only the most significant of which were covered here.

Future Glock

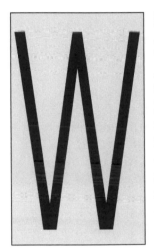

hen Glock pistols first came to America in the mid-1980s, they were greeted with mixed reviews. Acceptance came slowly at first, then grew with increasing rapidity. In those early days it was interesting to see who among firearms professionals took what position on the controversial pistols. Often even more interesting were some of the reasons and excuses offered in defense of the various stands taken.

But despite the world's current overwhelming acceptance of these marvelous pistols, there are, as there always will be, some who feel they must buck the tide. I'm not alluding here to those with legitimate design and/or application disagreements. No, I'm referring to the few who go out of their way to rationalize their vehement opposition as if it were a crusade—as if the burden of saving the world from Glocks rests heavily upon their shoulders and those of their few renegade compatriots.

I have absolutely no complaint with people who, for whatever genuine reasons, don't care for Glock pistols. My grievance is with those like the California Highway Patrol (which should know better, but nevertheless bases its decision against adopting Glocks on a bogus foundation) and one Michael D. Powers.

On page 26 of its 8 June 1991 issue, *The Boston Globe* ran an article about two Boston Police Department officers. An excerpt from that article:

> In a March 27 (1991) letter to Boston Police Commissioner Francis M. Roache, Michael D. Powers, the department's former counsel, said he managed to release the safety of the Glock with his pinky finger . . . Powers wrote the letter in his capacity as lawyer for officers Joseph Tate and Guy Bowens, who have been under investigation by the department's internal affairs division since Tate was critically wounded in the chest February 15th (1991) while he was in Bowen's Dorchester condominium. Tate, who has recovered, fired the gun accidentally. Powers asked Roache to investigate the Glock "before another Boston police officer discharges the weapon and either the officer or a member of the general public loses his life," Powers wrote.

Powers wrote that the Glock had two other serious defects: no lock to keep the magazine in place and, when the magazine is removed, a live round remains in the chamber. In addition, Powers wrote, "Quality weapons allow for the removal of the magazine without leaving behind a live round."

The learned Mr. Powers' concluding quote in the article was, "These killer assault weapons should be banned in Boston."

The merit of Mr. Powers' argument is reflected in its content. For example, suggesting that a pistol is defective because "it has no lock to keep the magazine in place and, when the magazine is removed a live round remains in the chamber" is absurd and serves only to highlight Powers' ignorance.

All modern pistols with removable magazines employ some sort of spring-loaded magazine-retention device which, when activated, permits magazine removal. The Glock design is substantially identical to all other "American-style" mechanisms, actuated by a button near the top left side of the grip.

If there was ever any uncertainty about the worthlessness of Powers' remarks or his lack of credibility, his notion that "quality weapons allow for the removal of the magazine without leaving behind a live round" should dispel all doubt. In fact, no pistols do what he suggests "quality weapons" do; there are no mechanisms that prevent magazine removal when there's a live round in the chamber, nor are there any that remove chambered rounds automatically when the magazine is removed.

Powers' characterization of Glocks as "killer assault weapons" is as inane as the rest of his remarks. Glocks are not assault weapons—they're defense weapons, as are virtually all handguns. Use of the word "killer" is inflammatory and divisive. Unfortunately, current state-of-the-art weapons technology requires that handguns be capable of killing in order to be effective for defense.

Glock pistols are as defect-free as any firearms available today, and far more so than most. Perhaps Mr. Powers should address his outrage to the real issues in Boston—such as why it appears some of the police officers have been playing fast and loose with the truth—before he publicly embarrasses himself further at Glock's expense.

The CHP, Michael D. Powers, and the lunatic fringe aside, it seems as if Glock's popularity continues to grow as impressively as ever. As of this writing (July 1991) all models were being shipped, but because of the overwhelming volume of orders, Glock personnel refused to speculate upon the timing of development of future

Glock models. Which leads us into the final question: what does the future hold for Glock firearms?

There will be a line of carbines. These will be produced in all the pistol calibers, with magazines interchanging between pistols and carbines of the same caliber. Executive VP Walter speculates that .40-caliber carbines will be the first to be introduced.

Walter also confirms that an ultracompact 9mm pistol is in the works. It will have a single-column magazine and will be designed for deep-cover-type concealment. It is unknown whether or not a .40-caliber pistol will be built on the same size frame.

Finally, there are rumors floating about that Glock will one day produce compact versions of its Models 20 and 21. These small renditions of the 10mm and .45 ACP pistols, so the rumors go, will be proportional to the Model 20/21 receiver as that of the Model 19/23 is to the Model 17/22 receiver.

So far these are unconfirmed rumors, but I wouldn't be surprised to see such things and more from the marvelous mind of Gaston Glock.

Resource List

Aftermarket Holsters

Alessi Holsters, Inc.
2465 Niagra Falls Blvd.
Tonawanda, NY 14150

BHF Police Equipment
427 Robinson Road
Cedartown, GA 30125

Bianchi International, Inc.
100 Calle Cortez
Temecula, CA 92390

Bob Mixon
7435 W. 19th Court
Hialeah, FL 33104

DeSantis Holsters & Leather Goods
140 Denton Ave.
New Hyde Park, NY 11040

Don Hume Leather Goods
P.O. Box 351
Miami, OK 74354

Galco International, Ltd.
4311 W. Van Buren
Phoenix, AZ 85043

George Lawrence Company
1435 NW Northrup
Portland, OR 97209

Gould & Goodrich
709 E. McNeil St.
Lillington, NC 27546

K.L. Null
678 Green Springs Road
Hanover, PA 17331

Milt Sparks
Box 187
Idaho City, ID 83631

Prezine Holsters
1736 St. Johns Bluff Road
Jacksonville, FL 32216

Safariland Leather
1941 S. Walker Ave.
Monrovia, CA 91016

Strong Holster Company
105 Maplewood Ave.
Gloucester, MA 01930

Aftermarket Magazines

U.S.A. Magazines (Clips)
Carlos Santizo
P.O. Box 39115
Downey, CA 90241

Competition Accessories & Modifications

JAF Gunsmithing, Inc.
José A. Fernandez
6435 S.W. 50th St.
Miami, FL 33155

Affirmative Safety

Sanco Guns
Nolan Santy
River Road
Bow, NH 03304

Training

Glock, Inc.
Al Bell, Director of Training
Frank DiNuzzo, Assistant Director of Training
P.O. Box 369
Smyrna, GA 30081
(factory training)

OffShoots Training Institute
Jerry and Cathy Lane
P.O. Box 719
Kennesaw, GA 30144
(contract training for Glock factory customers)

Police Training Division
Peter M. Tarley
2 Edgebrook Lane
Monsey, NY 10952
(contract training for Glock factory customers)

Peregrine Corporation
Emmanuel Kapelsohn
P.O. Box 170
Bowers, PA 19511
(contract training for Glock factory customers)

Threat Management Institute
Peggi Bird and Peter Kasler
800 West Napa St.
Sonoma, CA 95476
(Glock training courses for law enforcement and civilians)